# Withdrawn

READINGS
for a
MODERN
CHRISTMAS

# ALL I REALLY WANT

QUINN CALDWELL

*Nashville*

**All I Really Want**

Readings for a Modern Christmas

Copyright © 2014 by Quinn G. Caldwell

*Library of Congress Cataloging-in-Publication Data*

Caldwell, Quinn, 1977-
  All I really want : readings for a modern Christmas / Quinn G. Caldwell.
    pages cm
  ISBN 978-1-4267-9017-1 (binding: alk. paper)  1. Advent—Prayers and
devotions.  I. Title.
  BV40.C33 2014
  242'.33—dc23

                                                              2014034949

14 15 16 17 18 19 20 21 22 23—10 9 8 7 6 5 4 3 2 1

MANUFACTURED IN THE UNITED STATES OF AMERICA

*For Mom,*
*my first publisher*

# INTRODUCTION

**L**et's just get one thing straight: this book is not going to help you "simplify the season." It's not going to help you with the "Christmas time-crunch." It's not going to help you organize your holidays, throw a stress-free Christmas party, or create the Best Christmas Ever in five easy steps. If that's what you're looking for, I'm sure there's a *Special Double Holiday Bonus Issue!* of some trendy home magazine at the grocery store you can drop fifteen bucks on. (And if you do, will you grab me one? I love those things.)

I'm not here to simplify anything for you. Neither is God. If you have too many cookie exchanges or whatever, you're just going to have to find a way to deal with that yourself.

This book is actually designed to complicate the season. It's here to invite you to think and pray a little more deeply about it, not organize it all until it's easy. Here's how it works: for each day in December (roughly equivalent to the church season of Advent) and for the twelve days following Christmas (the church season of Christmastide), there's one reading for the morning and one for the evening. Each one consists of a Bible passage, a short reflection, and a prayer. Because action usually precedes belief, not the other way around, the reading will more often than not include a task for you to do, or at least a question to think about. There's also a calendar of small daily actions you can take, should you choose—small actions that all aim to help you make a little holy breathing space. Like everything else in the world, what you get out of these assignments will depend on what you put into them. So do it right.

The Christmas season is a time when churchgoers and non-churchgoers alike tend to experience strong spiritual long-ings. Whatever the longing looks like on the outside, for most of us, deep down it's a longing for an experience of something holy, something beautiful. Something like God. So although this book is here to add things to your to-do list, not to take them away, I hope that the doing of them will create room—maybe just enough room—for God to show up.

I don't know about you, but this year, that's all I really want.

ALL I
REALLY
WANT

# Christmas Calendar
## WEEK ONE

**1** Go get your Advent calendar. Start opening!

**2** Open the next door on your calendar. Stare at the others with longing. Don't cheat.

**3** Put a star in your room that you can see in the dark. Fall asleep staring at it.

**4** Call somebody fun and make plans for a favorite Christmas tradition: to bake a cookie, to sing a carol, or to trim a tree.

**5** Call somebody and say something rare and important to them.

**6** Find a recording of "Prepare Ye" from *Godspell* (check out iTunes and YouTube). Crank it up to 11 and dance around the house while singing it at the top of your lungs and throwing tinsel around.

**7** Turn out all the lights and relish the dark for a while tonight. Pray for gestation.

## December 1

Lead me in your truth—teach it to me—because you are the God who saves me. I put my hope in you all day long.
(Psalm 25:5)

Some days it seems like waiting is all you do. For the train. For a reply to your e-mail. For your lunch order. For somebody at the customer service center, which is "experiencing higher-than-normal call volume," to pick up the freaking phone. For the other shoe to drop. Some days it feels like everybody but you is in control of your time, and all you can do—even if they have *Highlights* magazine in the waiting room—is sit around hoping they'll get to you soon.

Apparently, the malls and stores feel pretty much the same way; these days, they put up their Christmas decorations before Halloween. I hate delayed gratification as much as the next guy, but the fact that all the big retailers seem to be against waiting is pretty much a guarantee that there must be some virtue in it.

So today, since you'll be doing so much of it anyway, see if you can discover the virtue in waiting. Try to pay attention whenever you find yourself sitting around. Don't stick your earphones in or take your book

# MORNING

out as soon as you get to the bus stop. Don't go for Angry Birds as soon as you get to the grocery line. Instead, notice: who's making you wait? Why? What are you waiting for? How important is it? Who's waiting with you? Why are you so impatient; is the next thing you have to do really so important? Why?

And most important of all: what are you *really* waiting for?

*OK, God. You know I'm no good at this waiting thing. But I know you are. So enter into my wait and liven things up. Amen.*

December 1

"There will be signs in the sun, moon, and stars. On the earth, there will be dismay among nations in their confusion over the roaring of the sea and surging waves. The planets and other heavenly bodies will be shaken, causing people to faint from fear and foreboding of what is coming upon the world. Then they...

...will see the Human One coming on a cloud with power and great splendor. Now when these things begin to happen, stand up straight and raise your heads because your redemption is near." (Luke 21:25-28)

There's waiting, and then there's waiting.

Sometimes it's the oh-God-when-will-this-pain-end kind of waiting. Sometimes it's just annoying, like waiting for your turn at the restroom. Sometimes it's worse, like waiting out the period after a gnarly divorce.

But there's another kind of waiting, too, a delicious, shivery kind: There's smelling the almost-done pie in the oven. There's sitting in the theater listening to the opening theme of a movie you've been waiting a year to see. There's feeling the baby kick you in the bladder a week before due date. There's lying in bed listening to your lover coming up the stairs.

Advent—those weeks leading up to Christmas—is about both kinds of waiting.

# EVENING

On the one hand, it's about looking around at the state of the world, at the wars and the climate and the corporations and the seasonal allergies, and longing for God to end the wait and show up already. It's about choosing to see God's absence.

On the other, it's about choosing to see God's almost-presence. It's about looking around at the state of the world, at the struggling schoolteachers and rich philanthropists doing the right thing, at the babies being born and the love being made and the ancient stars shining bright as hope in the cold night sky. It's about looking around at all of this, reading the signs, and knowing that everything is about to change.

Advent is about standing in the slop and calling, "How long, Lord?" But just as surely, it's about standing in the shining, shivering with delight and singing, "Come, Lord, come."

*Lord, this world needs you, bad. Fill it up with signs of your coming, signs so obvious even I can see them, and set me to work to welcome you. Amen.*

# December 2

*Teach us to number our days so we can have a wise heart.*
*(Psalm 90:12)*

I just love me a good Advent calendar. Growing up, we got new ones every year, carefully selected for each child. At the end of each day, we would open its corresponding door on the calendar. Some calendars had little pictures of Christmassy things behind the doors. Some were scratch-and-sniff. Some had candy in tiny compartments. Awesome.

Always, the biggest, most beautiful door on the whole calendar was the one marked "24." It was supposed to stay closed until Christmas Eve, when whatever cool thing it hid would be revealed. (Obviously, we always peeked.)

I remember the quiet wonder with which we opened each of those little doors, so much more tangible, so much more engaging than the sedate lighting of the four Advent candles in church. We weren't very good at saying grace at mealtimes, our bedtime rituals in those days had much more to do with toothbrushes than with prayers, and our longings had more to do with the

Sears Wish Book than with the redemption of the Creation. But we gathered around those little doors each night with the hushed expectancy that they told us we were supposed to feel in church. As we did, we learned something about waiting, about counting, about longing, and about God.

There are plenty of Advent calendars in the stores, plenty online, and of course there are apps for that (though those won't let you peek). Get on it.

*O Holy Mystery, you hide behind every door and peep from every window. In these days, grant that I might learn to pause, to hush, long enough to see you there. Amen.*

December 2

Another thing I like about Advent calendars: they dole Christmas out glimpse by glimpse. They build up the picture or the story in slow, random-seeming increments. They don't go all the way in one shot. They require pauses. They require little bursts of delight. They require patience.

Advent is about expecting the coming of Christmas, the remembrance of Jesus' first coming. But it's also about expecting Jesus' *second* coming, the one that he said would straighten up the world, delight the good, open the eyes of the bad, and fix everything. It's about sinking not only into the longing and trepidation of that promise but also into trust that it will be fulfilled.

Since the earliest days, believers and scoffers alike have been asking "Well, why isn't he back yet?" And they've wondered whether it might be that he's not coming back. The author of Second Peter has an answer for them: he's not back yet, dear Humankind, not because he's slow or uninterested or not coming at all, but because

# EVENING

he's giving *you* time to pull yourself together before he does. Time to practice seeing him in small ways so you'll recognize him when he arrives in big ones. He's revealing himself in slow, random-seeming increments, just little glimpses here and there of the picture he's painting, of the story whose end he is. It's your job to be patient, to pause, to look, to be prepared for little bursts of delight.

So why don't you go get to practicing and open that next door on the calendar?

*God, you've been gone a long time. The world is ready for you to come back now. But I assume you know what you're doing, so I guess we can wait till you're ready. In the meantime, don't leave us without a little preview now and then, OK? Amen.*

*Lord, you have been our dwelling place in all generations.*
*(Psalm 90:1 NRSV)*

Sometimes I think we ask too much of home. We load it up with more freight than any one word or idea or even place could ever manage. It's not only the place we came from; but it's also the place we're supposed to be welcome no matter what. It's supposed to be the container for all our soft-focus memories, all of who we used to be and used to hope we would become. It's supposed to smell like cookies baking and sound like laughter at old stories. It's the locus of so much nostalgia that it's no wonder it tends to collapse under the weight of all the expectations we load it with.

Maybe you're one of the luckier ones when it comes to home. But even if everyone there is well-adjusted, un-addicted, constantly healthy, and never resentful, even if it's still populated by all the dear ones who have been there since you were born, even if you love being there more than anywhere in the world, still it will never be what the made-for-TV movies want you to think it should be; still it's not likely to be all you remember or all you hope. The problem with home is that it's full of people, and whether it's full of their presence or their absence, at least one of them is probably going to annoy the crap out of you while you're there.

So what the psalmist has to say should be good news for just about everybody this Christmas, whether you're headed home for the holidays or have no home to speak of, trapped far from home or planning to host the gathering, or looking forward to or dreading whatever reunions are in your imminent future.

Because all that we ask of home that it can't deliver, all that we depend on it for that it disappoints us in, all that we need and it will never be able to deliver? Your home can't deliver it, but God can, and the porch light is on.

So today, look around at the home you're in now. Change one thing in it to make it more like what a home ought to be: clean some old baggage out of a closet, invite a friend over to fill it up with love, rearrange a shelf to make it more beautiful, or go to the grocery store and pay a little more to buy the fair-trade option of whatever you're getting. Make just one small change, and dedicate it to God.

*God, you are my refuge and my might, my alpha and omega. You are my true home. Which is a good thing, since the one I have in this world is so weird. Amen.*

*I'm the root and descendant of David, the bright morning star.
(Revelation 22:16)*

Why is everything scarier in the middle of the night? A noise you wouldn't think twice about if you heard it at noon can paralyze you at 2 A.M. A dream you'd totally just laugh off during your afternoon nap leaves you staring at the ceiling, blankets up to your chin, in the wee hours. A window that has never looked out on anything but the side yard becomes the potential frame for a vision of horror when you're on your way for your midnight pee.

And that's just for those of us who live in relatively safe houses. Never mind those who spend their nights on subway grates or cardboard, in fear of attack or invasion, in danger of spouses or temptation.

So what is it? Is it that at night, we're more vulnerable or just feel more vulnerable? Is it that the dangers are greater or just look bigger in the dark?

Against the shadows, against the night, against that which stalks the good and the bad, for those who live their lives in night-times of fear and for those who just wake

# EVENING

up alone once in a while, Jesus promises this: the night will end. The morning star will rise, and then the sun. The night will not and cannot finally win.

If you find that easy to believe in the daytime, but a little harder at night, hang a star in your room this Advent, a light-up Christmas star from Target, a glow-in-the-dark star stuck on the ceiling, or a starry night-light. You can call it a Christmas decoration so your friends don't think you're weird, if you want. But don't forget what it really is: a promise.

*Lord, I don't know how long this night is going to be. But with you, I know it's going to end. Come, Morning Star, come. Amen.*

## December 4

*Therefore says the Sovereign, the LORD of hosts, the Mighty One of Israel: . . . I will smelt away your dross as with lye and remove all your alloy. (Isaiah 1:24-25 NRSV)*

The Israelites have been worshiping other gods alongside their own. They have created what God, in the mouth of Isaiah, calls an "alloy" religion. Isaiah and the other ancient prophets were always worrying about purity of faith and worship; any mixing, they fretted, would bring the whole thing to its knees. To hear them tell it, God agreed.

I sometimes have a similar reaction to Christmas, to our frenetic, consumerist interpretation of its meaning, to all those catalogues and Very Special Episodes of TV shows. Sometimes, it seems to me an unholy alloy.

But then I tell myself to lighten up. I mean, is every alloy bad? And mightn't God be powerful enough to co-opt the culture's co-optation of the day of his birth? I think God can work with the traditions we hand to God.

In that Spirit, here are some Christmas things that have nothing to do with Jesus' birth, but in which I believe God is at work anyway:

❄ *Elvis's Christmas Album.* If it can make my whole family sing together while performing a complex operation involving a saw, a tree, a small living room, electricity, and water without us killing one another, it's holy.

❄ Shopping. Yes, it can get out of hand, but searching for a great gift to make someone happy can be a profound experience.

❄ *Emmet Otter's Jug-Band Christmas.* In fact, Christmas specials in general—especially if they're commercial-free.

❄ Your favorite. What traditions or celebrations do you love? What do they teach you about God? Have you made your plans for doing them yet this year?

*God, you can make anything holy. Bless my celebrations when they increase my love, make me generous, or open me to your world. If they do the opposite, make them go the way of last year's fruitcake. Amen.*

...The people of Nineveh will rise up at the judgment with this generation and condemn it, because they changed their hearts and lives in response to Jonah's preaching—and one greater than Jonah is here. (Luke 11:31-32)

[Jesus said,] The queen of the South will rise up at the judgment with the people of this generation and condemn them, because she came from a distant land to hear Solomon's wisdom. And look, someone greater than Solomon is here....

Jesus isn't as concerned with being Christmassy as you might think he would be. Sometimes, he is positively not in the holiday spirit. What about peace and goodwill to all? Talking stable animals and cuddly babies? Miraculous stars and angel choirs? Why you gotta harsh our mellow?

I'd hate to try to speak for Jesus, but I think if he were here, he'd say something like, "Yeah, but if you believe all that stuff happened, even if you believe it happened 'metaphorically'"—I imagine him gritting his teeth a little and making air quotes on that last word—"then can you please explain the state of the world? Can you explain to me why you did what you did last Tuesday? If you believe all that stuff is true about me and about what God did, can you explain, oh, I don't know . . . *Duck Dynasty*?"

Everybody always talks about how busy they get around Christmastime. You'd think with all those Christians going full steam ahead for a month, the world would take a giant step forward at the end of every year, that the planet would lurch a little closer to paradise each December. That it doesn't seem to work that way *might* suggest that we're not busy with exactly the right things.

So how about this: take some time right now, here at the beginning of Advent, and add a holy something to your to-do list. A volunteer gig. A sizable donation to a good charity. A visit to your ailing aunt. A little political action. It won't save the world, but it'll be a start.

*Lord, take from me the busy-ness that does not signify, and fill my calendar up with work to save the world. Because the Queen of Sheba has been dead for a long time, and I do not want to meet her face to face. Amen.*

**December 5**

John's father Zechariah was filled with the Holy Spirit and prophesied, "Bless the Lord God of Israel because [God] has come to help and has delivered [God's] people. (Luke 1:67-68)

So God tells Zechariah, who's really old, that he's about to have a son and that he should name that son John. Zechariah doubts that he and his equally old wife are going to manage such a feat. God tells him that he will be struck silent until the promise is fulfilled. When his wife, Elizabeth, gives birth and people ask them what the name will be, Zechariah writes, "His name is John," on a tablet. Suddenly, his voice is freed. And his first words? One of the most beautiful songs of the Bible. The Benedictus, named for the Latin translation of its first word, later came to be recited at morning prayer by Christians the world round in the hopes that, by saying what Zechariah had said, their tongues, too, would be freed for praise each day.

Have you ever been silenced by what you didn't dare say aloud? And did you one day find enough strength or faith or dire need to say it? And when you said it, did you find yourself unlocked, your voice loosed for prayer and praise, your life freed like a stone rolled away from a tomb?

What was it you said?

Was it, "I'm gay"?

"My husband hits me"?

"I love you"?

"I'm an alcoholic"?

"Will you marry me"?

"I'm not going to take it any more"?

"I believe in God"?

"Please forgive me"?

For Zechariah, it was, "His name is John." For Mary, it was, "I'm pregnant."

If you haven't said yours yet, what are you waiting for?

*Blessed be you, O God. Give me words like keys, and free my life for faith and praise. Amen.*

**December 5**

*You, child, will be called a prophet of the Most High, for you will go before the Lord to prepare his way. You will tell his people how to be saved through the forgiveness of their sins. (Luke 1:76-77)*

Zechariah stops dead in the middle of his grand Benedictus, mercifully stops declaiming, and instead starts singing to Baby John. Picture him, the great priest and prophet, turning from his audience to his son, switching from oratory to lullaby, public to private. Picture him stroking his son's face and choking up as he sings these words to him.

For my money, the image of this crotchety old priest singing to his boy is as tender and arresting a scene as a Madonna and child, all the more poignant for knowing where the tiny head resting in the crook of that bony arm would wind up in the end. (If you don't know, Google John the Baptist to find out.)

That Luke recorded this song in such detail can only mean that it was intended to be used, said, and sung to other babies. Not everybody can be Jesus. But anybody can be John. Anybody can point to Jesus, tell the world that the dawn is on its way, get a glimpse of God on the road, and yell, "Everybody! Look over there!"

# EVENING

Apparently, Luke thought God wanted lots of other fathers to sing this song to lots of other babies besides John. I don't know if you're as lucky in your father as John was in his; too many people aren't. But even if you aren't, that doesn't mean God's not singing it to you anyway.

So before you go to bed tonight, take a few minutes to think about your day. Come up with one place—just one!—where you saw the hand of God at work. If you get stuck, look in the mirror.

*Holy God, let me relax into your arms and into your lullaby. I'm not sure I have what it takes to be a prophet, but show yourself to me, and I will tell the world. Amen.*

# December 6

They asked, "Where is the newborn king of the Jews? We've seen his star in the east, and we've come to honor him."
(Matthew 2:2)

Is there anybody else out there who hates tasteful Christmas decorations? Who's appalled by genteel ornamentation? Who, when faced with a color-coordinated Christmas tree covered in matching ornaments, has to fight off the urge to set it on fire just to liven things up a little?

I mean, this is *Christmas* we're talking about, people! *Christmas*! The day that unto us a child was born? The day that made all of heaven sing in wonderment and joy? The day the Creator of the cosmos *entered history and changed it for-freaking-ever*?

This calls for tinsel.

It calls for projects made in first grade, with gobs of hardened glue and glitter. It calls for colored lights—big colored lights, ideally with water bubbling in them. It calls for motorized tree stands and blinking stars and construction paper chains and singing ornaments.

Christmas is not a day for restraint; it's a day for blowing the doors off their hinges. I'm not saying you *have* to decorate your house. I'm just saying that if you're going to decorate it, you best make it look like a party. When God decided to decorate for Christmas, God hung an enormous star in the heavens, not a string of demure white lights. No doubt the neighbors were appalled, but it sure did draw a crowd.

So today, celebrate the God who didn't hold back anything. Be unrestrained. Put on some music, loud, and start decorating. Make it look like a *party* up in here, and praise God's holy name.

*God, grant that I might decorate my life so outrageously that wise ones come from all around to learn what I know about you. Amen.*

### December 6

*The light shines in the darkness, and the darkness doesn't extinguish the light. (John 1:5)*

I know what I said a couple of days ago about decorations and about the night-time being scary, but still, sometimes all the light can get to be a bit much this time of year: blinking lights, bubble lights, icicle lights, blue-light specials. What about those of us who like the dark sometimes? You know, those of us who like to sit outside at night, who relish sitting in a dim bar sharing a drink with a friend, who appreciate a snuggle with the lights off.

For those of us living in modern, industrialized societies, where everything is spotlighted or fluoresced to within an inch of its life, dimness can be hard to come by.

God shined bright when he entered the world, but it couldn't have happened without the holy darkness of Mary's womb, without the darkness behind the closed eyelids of a laboring woman, without the darkness of the space between a baby's skin and swaddle.

# EVENING

The wise men would never have been able to see that star if they'd been standing in the parking lot of a twenty-four-hour Walmart.

So tonight, in honor of the good darkness, the holy darkness, spend some time with the lights off. Look out at the world or just at the backs of your eyelids. Pray to be protected and nourished and formed by the God who swept over the face of the waters before there was light. Pray for the darkness to become like the womb that bore the world. Pray for gestation. Pray for birth.

*God, thank you for light and dark, bright and dim. Whether I am in shining or in shadow, let me show you to the world. Amen.*

I rejoiced with those who said to me,
"Let's go to the LORD's house!"
(Psalm 122:1)

Funny thing about this time of year: suddenly, everybody wants to go to church. Say, "Let us go to the house of the Lord," in December, and all the world's your friend. Say it in the middle of July, and all the world rolls its eyes at you as it heads out to the beach.

Even you. I bet we'll see you at church on Christmas Eve, even if we never see you any other time.

Why is that? Why that night instead of some other? Yeah, your mom made you go, I know. But she tries to get you to go lots of other times, and it doesn't work then. Why this holiday and not some other one?

Just what is it about this time of year that makes people start going to church more? Is it habit? Some ingrained cultural thing? Are we making up for lost time? Is it because the children's programs ramp up? Or because we really like the music? Or because the parents of the world really double down on their wheedling?

Or is there something about lengthening nights and colder days and death in the garden? Isn't there something—some need or fear or longing—that shrinks away in the long hot sun by the pool but which grows as fall turns to winter, until even you can feel it? That becomes large and threatening in the backseat when you're driving home from work in full dark at 6 p.m?

Now's a good time of year to find a churchgoer you know and get him or her to invite you to a service. And if you are a churchgoer, keep a lookout for a friend who might be nudging for an invite.

Because this time of year might come as something of a relief (even though you pretend it doesn't) when someone says, "Let's go to church." Because don't you know that there lies reassurance that whatever it is following you around in the backseat, there's no way it's going to beat you to Bethlehem?

*God, let me long for you summer and winter, light and dark, and let me always be glad when someone invites me to visit you. Amen.*

December 7

*"What do you think? A man had two sons. Now he came to the first and said, 'Son, go and work in the vineyard today.' 'No, I don't want to,' he replied. But later he changed his mind and went." (Matthew 21:28-32)*

By now, regular churchgoers out there will have noticed the pews in your church beginning to fill up. If your church is like mine, attendance will continue to grow right up through Christmas Eve, when your sanctuary will be fuller than at any other time, except maybe Easter.

You people who don't get to church that often will find yourselves making an extra effort to show up in the next few weeks. If you don't go often enough the rest of the year to have a regular pew, you might slip into the back row. Maybe somebody will recognize you; maybe not. Maybe you'll care; maybe not.

Regular worshipers will rejoice in all the extra people; they also might be tempted to look cynically at the C&E (Christmas and Easter) Christians with whom they suddenly find themselves sharing their pews.

Against any who would be too hard on those who only manage to make it to church on the big days, Jesus tells this parable. One son says he won't go work in the vineyard when their father asks, but then he does it. Another son says he'll go but then doesn't. Even Jesus' adversaries have to admit that it's the first son who does the father's will.

C&E Christians may not make it to church much, but Jesus points out that God cares more about what we do out in the vineyard than about what we do when the authorities are looking. Who knows what miracles of grace were born this year through that guy sitting next to you whom you haven't seen since last April?

This year, if you're an every-Sunday type, give C&E church-goers a break. Welcome them without cynicism. Thank God for bringing you together. Be sure to invite them back.

And if you're a C&E type, or one of those lightning-will-strike-if-I-set-foot-in-a-church type, don't slink into the back row; walk in like you belong there because you do.

*God, however often I find myself in church, help me act like I'm yours when I'm outside it, too. Amen.*

# Christmas Calendar
## WEEK TWO

**8** Amp up your churchgoing for Advent. If you have a church, show up more than you usually would. If you don't have one, do a little work on Google and find a few to try out in the coming weeks.

**9** Bring something to life today: plant some seeds in anticipation of the spring.

**10** Read Revelation 21–22 (find it online if you don't have a Bible—bible.oremus.org is a good place to start). Let one thing you do today be an echo of that future.

**11** Go shopping for a present to send to someone, and just sign the package "Santa."

**12** Set a timer for thirty minutes, call or sit down with someone you respect, and wonder together why Jesus came.

**13** Instigate something good today, even if it's just a batch of brownies for the postal worker.

**14** Write down five things that you saw or experienced this week that remind you of God.

# December 8

I like atheists. They tend to have considered the issues. They tend to have asked themselves the holy questions about the origins of the universe, about happiness, about what constitutes the good life, about good and evil, about injustice and mercy, and about how to live.

Of course they and I disagree on at least one fundamental point. Of course many are grumpy, judgmental, and dogmatic (certain public intellectuals come to mind). Of course many have chosen atheism out of laziness. Then again, those things are true of many Christians, as well. Sometimes, they're true of me.

By and large, my experience has been that the average atheist has arrived at her position through careful thinking at some cost to herself and lives a life marked by kindness and generosity, which is saying something in a world where many people's vision of the good life is spending half their time watching TV and the other half shopping—precisely so they don't have to think about big questions or make sacrifices.

Paul wanted to convince Jewish believers that God is at work everywhere, transforming lives even among persons who were not practicing Jews. Most of them wouldn't thank me for saying so, but I believe that's true for atheists, too: God is working through their best intentions, their brilliant thoughtfulness, their selfless love, and their attempts to be fair and to do the right thing.

My take is this: if what Paul says is true, then God is shown forth more fully in the life of a careful-thinking, good-living atheist than in that of a lukewarm Christian-by-default. If what Paul says is true, God might even prefer the former to the latter.

*God, thank you for working through all kinds of strange people—even me. Amen.*

December 8

The psalmist invites us to imagine God as a mother bird (those who insist on the maleness of God, take note!) spreading her wings over a nest filled to the brim with everybody in the world. The writer then goes on to mix the metaphor: God becomes the great high hostess, providing abundant food and drink to the world, gathered in her house.

But actually, the psalmist doesn't say that the whole world is there; just that the whole world *could* be there. Not that all people *do* take refuge in the shadow of God's wings; just that they *may*. Not that everybody loves going over to God's for dinner; just that they're invited.

Before that happens, before everybody in the world shows up in this way, somebody needs to tell them some stuff. Somebody needs to tell them that God is a mother hen calling her chicks home to safety, not a sharp-eyed hawk waiting to devour anybody who strays too far away. Somebody needs to tell them that God is a

# EVENING

hostess who just *loves* a houseful of guests, not a gatekeeper trying to keep everybody out. Before the whole world can show up in God's nest or God's dining room, somebody's going to need to tell them the truth.

Do you know someone who's been fed a whole line of false stories about God? Who's been told that God is cruel or is out to get them or doesn't know how to party or is just waiting to send them to hell? Who thinks he doesn't believe in any god at all but maybe really just doesn't believe in one specific God they heard some crazy dude on TV describing? Somebody who might sigh with delight to discover that God not only loves them fiercely and protectively but also knows how to throw an epic party?

If so, what are you going to do about it?

*God, continue to reveal yourself to me in new and surprising ways. And when you finally get me to understand, then grant me the boldness, the loudness, and the grace to tell the whole wide world and bring them home. Amen.*

## December 9

The desert and the dry land will be glad; the wilderness will rejoice and blossom like the crocus. They will burst into bloom.

(Isaiah 35:1-2)

The world was a desert for their love. Church and state had joined forces to make sure it wouldn't even sprout. But God is stronger than the desert. So Mildred Jeter, who was black, and Richard Loving, who was white, fell in love even though they lived in 1960s Virginia. And when discovered they were pregnant, they decided to get married—against all the anti-race mixing laws of convention and the state in that time and place. Eventually, what they did led to a US Supreme Court decision that struck down laws against interracial marriage throughout the country. The Lovings may not have quite done things in the "proper" order, but God made love flower in the desert.

The world was a desert for their love. Church and state had joined forces to make sure it wouldn't even sprout. But God is stronger than the desert. So same-sex couples fell in love anyway. Had children anyway. If they were lucky enough to be part of a religious tradition that loves them as much as they love each other, they got married anyway. Now in more and more places, such marriages are legal, and the flowers are overwhelming the desert.

The world should have been a desert for them, too. She was young, and pregnant by an unknown party. This apparent betrayal should have withered their love to the roots. But God is stronger than that, and so were Mary and Joseph. So they were married anyway, and life overwhelmed the world.

Once, nobody could imagine Abraham and Sarah having children; now we're all their descendants. Once, light-skinned and dark-skinned people getting together was unthinkable; now, the President of the United States is a product of such a family. Once, gay and lesbian people having children together boggled the mind; now I'm figuring out who should hold the baby while the couple is exchanging rings. Once, an illegitimate kid from Nazareth saving the world would have been laughable. But you know what happened then.

With our God, the desert never wins—especially not the desert we create for other people. With our God, love wins. With our God, life wins. So go bring something to life today. Water that plant that's almost gone, restart the book you started but forgot to finish, call up a friend you haven't talked to in years, go back to the gym, ask your lover to marry you, and praise God's name.

*O holy God, let me always trust that with you, barrenness and lifelessness are never, ever the end. Amen.*

December 9

*... prophesying, then a great quaking, and the bones came together, bone by bone.... I prophesied just as [God] commanded me. When the breath entered them, they came to life and stood on their feet, an extraordinarily large company. (Ezekiel 37:1, 7, 10)*

*The Lord's power overcame me, and while I was in the Lord's spirit, [God] led me out and set me down in the middle of a certain valley. It was full of bones.... I prophesied just as I was commanded. There was a great noise as I was...*

Here's what the story says: dry bones are not the final state of things. Death will not win. Here's what it says: life wins.

Here's what it doesn't say: that they were human bones. Or that those bones went back together in their original order. Or that the bodies at the end were the same as the bodies in the beginning.

We tell this story as if it's only about humans, as if we're the only species God loves enough to waste the energy on. But this is the God who notes the fall of every sparrow, right? Surely God noted the fall of every pterodactyl. Surely, God noticed the fate of the hominid

## EVENING

*Australopithecus afarensis* just as fully as God does that of the hominid *Homo sapiens*.

Ninety-nine percent of all the different species that once lived are now extinct. And yet, the place is full of life. Why? Because God does not let extinction win. The dinosaurs go down to bones and molecules, and the mammals rise up to take their place. *Homo habilis* goes extinct, and up rises *Homo sapiens*. One very particular *Homo sapiens*, soon to be born in Bethlehem, goes down to dust and rises up the king of heaven.

Death happens, but so does resurrection. Extinction happens, but so does evolution. And if our bones fit together differently when we walk out of the valley than when we walked in, maybe that's not so bad. I mean, you're better looking than *Paranthropus boisei* any day.

*For evolution, thank you. For resurrection, thank you. For not giving me a protruding brow ridge and shallow brain pan, thank you, thank you, thank you. Amen.*

## December 10

One of my favorite things about all the rituals and traditions attached to this time of year is the way they mess with time.

My husband and son and I decorate our Christmas tree, and as we hang each ornament—the ones we brought from our parents' houses and the ones we got together—we tell their stories. As we do, we find that we are not just standing in the living room we share, but we're also standing in footed pajamas in the living rooms we grew up in, decorating every tree we've ever decorated, right in that moment.

We gather on Christmas Eve with the lights down and the candles lit, and we sing "Silent Night." As we do, it's like we're singing it at every Christmas Eve service we've ever been to; it's like we're singing it at every Christmas Eve service yet to come; it's like, by our song, we're calling the birth of God into existence again.

It's not nostalgia; it's not just a hazy remembrance of the time back when things used to be better than they are now. It's more than that; it's like a collapsing of time, a drawing in of past and future into one long now.

Theologians would say we're stepping out of ordinary time, or what they call *chronos*, and catching a glimpse of God's time, or what they call *kairos*. In *chronos*, minute follows minute, and you can only go forward; that's where we live most of the time. But for God, in *kairos*, every moment is one, and your first Christmas, your last Christmas, this Christmas and the redemption of the whole world are all happening right now, forever.

It's one of the reasons people love this time of year so much, that quality it has that, for many people more than any other time of the year, lets us glimpse the world the way God sees it. So what things or traditions do that for you? What brings you back to your childhood at warp speed? Whatever it is, you should plan to do it soon.

*God, grant that the rituals and the songs and the traditions of this season might become for me passageways that lead me right into your heart. Amen.*

December 10

*Then the angel showed me the river of life-giving water, shining like crystal, flowing from the throne of God and the Lamb through the middle of the city's main street. On each side of the river is the tree of life . . . (Revelation 22:1)*

I had a pretty good childhood. For the most part, as kids, my sisters and I were happy, and as far as I can remember, all my childhood Christmases were happy ones. So when I get my Christmas on as an adult, I'm glad for that sense of the collapsing of time, the past intruding powerfully on the now. For me, it makes the now shinier.

The first time I realized that everybody might not love Christmas was when Billy's girlfriend, Kate, told about her dad dying in the chimney while pretending to be Santa in the movie *Gremlins*. Remember that one? Since then I've heard plenty of true stories almost as bad. What do you do when the smell of pine trees makes you remember getting hit? When "Jingle Bells" reminds you of somebody dying?

I suppose one thing you can do is avoid whatever the trigger is. Another might be to work on creating as many good Christmas memories as you can, to help balance the bad ones. I bet your therapist has even better suggestions than those.

# EVENING

And there's this: when you step out of *chronos* and into *kairos*, not only is it the past that comes rushing into the present; but it's the future, too. And whether you believe it or not, God has promised that the future will be beautiful. So go read the last chapter in the Bible, Revelation 22 (you can look it up online if you don't have a Bible lying around). Savor it. Then, as you decorate your tree, let it be not just the tree from your childhood, but the tree of the river of life as well. As you hang your lights, let them be the lights that will light the great wedding in heaven. As you sing your songs, let them be the angel choir singing you home triumphant. As you cook and as you eat, let it be the heavenly feast.

It won't fix everything, but having a vision of where you're going is the best way to leave where you're from.

*God, if I have to live with this past, I'm going to live with your future, too. Show it to me, and make me believe it. Amen.*

**December 11**

Not long ago, a friend of mine was at the drugstore with her small son, printing out pictures of their recent trip to visit Santa Claus. A woman standing nearby in sensible shoes (my friend didn't mention the shoe part, but I'm sure it has to be true; it always is with people like this) eyed the Santa photos and said, "So what are you going to do about the Big Lie? Do you have a therapist lined up for your son yet?"

I don't know a thing about Sensible Shoe Lady, but in my experience, the vast majority of people who make comments like this don't just think Santa's a bad idea; they think religion is a bad idea, too. Sure, there are a few loud "Santa = Satan" Christians out there, but that's not who you run into most of the time. (Pro tip: if you do meet some, point out to them that if rearranging the letters in *Santa* means something important, then surely rearranging the letters in *God* will lead to sound theology as well).

Here's what Santa does: Teaches

kids about dwelling in mystery. Shows them something about wonder. Encourages them to believe in things that are impossible *and* too beautiful not to be true. Hones their capacity for trusting in miracles. Sharpens their ability to trust, even through the fear that they might only get coal, that in the end, what they receive will be something good, something worth having. Yes, yes, Sensible Shoe Lady: all of these things can get out of hand later in life and cause all sorts of problems if you don't balance them with hard thinking, intellectual rigor, and science. But all of these things are all also part and parcel of faith.

And if the Santa in your house is careful, thoughtful, and discerning, the kids just might also learn this: you don't get every single thing you want in this life, but with our God, you will eventually get the one thing you really want.

If you don't have kids in your house, then spend today thinking about a kid whom you know and love. Get her or him a little present—it doesn't have to be big, just fun—send it from Santa, and never admit it was from you.

*God, help me help my kids believe in the most impossible wonder of all: how much you love the world, grumpy old Sensible Shoe Lady included. Amen.*

Part of what makes Santa Claus so wonderful is the building excitement, the looking-forward, the anticipation. But an even bigger part is the surprise. It's the wide-eyed delight of coming down the stairs or around the corner and discovering that someone had been thinking of you, had aimed for your happiness, and had gone to the trouble of bringing you what they thought you would love.

So how about playing Santa for someone who isn't expecting it this year? I don't mean the dreary old Secret Santa game that somebody at your office is forcing you to participate in. I mean really surprising the pants off a person who doesn't know it's coming. Who do you know who could use a little unexpected delight? Who do you know who would never think you'd get her something? Who could use a shot of wonder, a bit of beautiful mystery in the shape of an unsigned parcel in his mailbox? Is it the old lady across the street? The quiet guy in the lunchroom? The crotchety sales clerk

# EVENING

at the store? What do you know about each of them? What can you imagine about what he or she would love?

Think hard about it. Pray over it. Wonder about it. Consider coming up with the right thing to be as fun a game as stuffing a child's stocking. Then get it, create it, bake it, whatever. Go into stealth mode to get it into the person's hands. Don't sign the card. Don't get caught.

Trust that the finding of your gift will be a wide-eyed delight. Trust that it has the power to crack open a crusty heart, improve a terrible day, and help someone who's out of practice to believe in miracles. Believe that it's in your power to inject wonder into the world. Hope that what you've done has made a place, even just a little one, for God to enter in.

*God, I know that this whole Santa thing is just a game, but I believe it's a holy one. So I offer it up to you. Now do your thing. Amen.*

# December 12

*The snake...said to the woman, "Did God really say that you shouldn't eat from any tree in the garden?" The woman said to the snake, "We may eat the fruit of the garden's trees but not the fruit of the tree in the middle of the garden. ...*

*...God said, 'Don't eat from it, ...or you will die.'" The woman saw that the tree was beautiful with delicious food and that the tree would provide wisdom, so she took some of its fruit and ate it, and also gave some to her husband...and he ate it. (Genesis 3:1-3, 6)*

Here's how some people tell the story: Adam and Eve broke the rules way back in the Garden of Eden. God punished them in all sorts of ways—mostly by allowing death to enter the world. The stain of this original sin is passed to each new generation through the sexual union of the parents, and each new baby is born deserving to die. God eventually felt bad about this or something and "graciously" decided to offer a way out. So God came to us in Jesus Christ and made of Godself a sacrifice on the cross. This was because only the spilling of God's blood was powerful enough to wash that original sin away. So now, everybody's still born deserving to die, but at least there's an out in the form of Jesus Christ, if you want to take it. If not, enjoy hell!

Nope.

Nope nope nope nope nope nope nope.

I dare you to try to tell this story while holding a newborn baby. I dare you to look into that baby's eyes and say, "You are stained and deserve to die." If you can't bring yourself to do that, then I for one think you ought to find a different way to tell the story of Jesus.

If we don't tell the story this way, though, then what way should we tell the story? Why did Jesus need to come? *Did* he need to come? What was the point? What difference did it make?

Take some time today to wonder about these questions. More important, take some time to pray about them. Ask somebody you trust what they think. Set aside some real time—a good half hour at least—and wonder.

*God, I know that on this side of heaven, I'm never going to know the whole truth about what you were doing on Christmas. But if you could just give me enough to be getting on with, that would be great. Thank you. Amen.*

## December 12

God so loved the world that [God] gave [God's] only Son, so that everyone who believes in him won't perish but will have eternal life. God didn't send [the] Son into the world to judge the world, but that the world might be saved through him. (John 3:16-17)

How about this, instead? We're not totally depraved; we're just idiots, and we're way more helpless than any of us wants to admit.

How about this? We're capable of great things, but we're all screwups, too. Sure, some of us may be deeply sinful, even broken. But mostly, we're just huge dorks, lurching around and making messes while trying to do our best.

How about this? We almost never have all the information, so lots of our decisions suck.

How about this? We are to God as a two year old is to a well-adjusted parent.

How about this? We're easily distracted by shiny things and tend to wander off if you don't keep an eye on us.

How about this? God loves us not in spite of all this but because of it, because of the sheer depth of our goofiness and ultimate helplessness. Sometimes, all this really makes God mad; sometimes, it cracks God up. Eventually, God got tired of hollering down to us from upstairs to tell us to please stop fighting and just keep it to a dull roar. So Godself finally came down to break it up, to play with us a little, to give us some attention, to have some skin-contact time, and to see if he couldn't find something constructive for us to do.

How about this? God so loved the world that God wasn't about to let anything—not distance or our distraction, not danger or our disinterest, not our fractiousness or foolishness, and not even the threat of death itself—keep God away from us.

How about this? It's not about how good or bad we are. It's about how good God is.

*God, thank you for not leaving us down here trying to figure it out on our own. Amen.*

# December 13

*When the disciples arrived on the other side of the lake, they had forgotten to bring bread. Jesus said to them, "Watch out and be on your guard for the yeast of the Pharisees and Sadducees." They discussed this among ...*

*...themselves and said, "We didn't bring any bread." Jesus knew what they were discussing and said, "You people of weak faith! ..."* (Matthew 16:5-8)

In this story, we learn an important thing: overly literal people annoy Jesus.

After some rather testy remediation, the disciples learn what the reader of the story knows all along: Jesus is speaking in metaphors. He's not talking about *actual* yeast here; he's talking about bad ideas that spread like yeast.

Jesus speaks in metaphor a lot because he knows that pulsing under and through everything we see and experience is the life and power of God. Breaking through every moment of every day, just below the surface, is the realm of God, the future shaping the here and now. Empirical observation cannot detect it. Objective testing will not uncover it. Literalism can never apprehend it. It is usually not obvious. The best we can do is to feel it and then to talk about it in simile and metaphor.

I think that overly literal people annoy Jesus because they miss the God and the grace that are all around them. They look at the story of Jesus' birth, and they see two people trying to cover up some extramarital hanky-panky and an unexpected pregnancy with stories of angels and miracles. They look at bread and cup, and they see ... bread and cup. They look at the cross and see ... two pieces of wood. They look at a newborn baby and see ... carbon. It is a dreary way to move through the world.

So today, practice seeing in metaphors. Look deeper than the surface. Try to see the world deeply, as Jesus sees it: full of God. Today, commit to not being a literalist.

*O God, teach me to look deep, to see your power coursing through the world. And in the looking, bring me closer to you. Amen.*

*During the journey, as he approached Damascus, suddenly a light from heaven encircled him. For three days he was blind and neither ate nor drank anything. (Acts 9:3, 9)*

You might know this story. After Jesus' death, this guy Saul is going around persecuting Jesus' followers. Then the story in Acts 9 happens (and he hears the voice of God basically telling him to cut it out), and afterward he becomes Paul, one of Jesus' biggest fans.

The Wikipedia article about Saul's conversion includes a researcher's claim that the experience sounded like "an attack of temporal lobe epilepsy, perhaps ending in a convulsion, which was startling and dramatic. The blindness which followed may have been post-ictal."

Some people have too much time on their hands.

Like those people who spend all their time trying to explain the ten plagues in Egypt or the parting of the Red Sea in terms of bacteria and windstorms. I mean, who cares if the event was scientifically explainable or something "supernatural"? Would it really be a surprise to learn that God can turn even earthquakes and epilepsy to good ends? As if something with a scientific explanation can't be an act of grace!

So many of the stories that go with this time of year are miraculous: virgin births, angelic appearances, psychic dreams, and traveling stars. You might be tempted to try to explain them rationally. Get over it.

Miracle stories aren't *supposed* to be explainable. Or, more to the point, they're not supposed to be explained. The right questions for a miracle, especially a miracle in Advent, don't start with *how* and *whether*. They start with *why* and, more important, *so what*. Don't look for explanation; look for meaning. Don't look for data; look for symbol. Don't look for facts; look for truth.

*God, I know you gave me a brain because you want me to use it. And I'll think super critically about all these stories in January, I promise. But for now, help me get so lost in the miracles that I find my way to you. Amen.*

# December 14

When Jesus was at Bethany visiting the house of Simon, who had a skin disease, a woman came to him with a vase made of alabaster containing very expensive perfume. She poured it on Jesus' head while he was sitting at dinner. Now when the disciples saw it they...said, "Why this waste? ...

...This perfume could have been sold for a lot of money and given to the poor." But Jesus knew what they were thinking. He said, "Why do you make trouble for the woman? She's done a good thing for me. I tell you the truth that wherever in the whole world this good news is announced, what she's done will also be told in memory of her." (Matthew 26:6-10, 13)

I swear, if one more person drops one more sanctimonious lecture on me about how terrible Christmas shopping is for the world, I'm going to blow my next paycheck on plastic junk from Walmart and send it to the lecturer just to make that person mad.

It's like in today's story. The disciples were obviously right here. They'd been listening to Jesus, and they knew what the faithful do with their money: give it away. They knew what the faithful do with rich things: sell them and give the money to the poor. They were only following what Jesus had told them.

However, they were using his words as a weapon, and that just never sits well with Jesus. When the letter of the law gets in the way of the Spirit of praise, when the rules are used to elevate oneself over others, when those who love God so much they can't help it get beaten down by those who are and must always be "right," Jesus gets mad. Against those whose following of commandments gets in the way of their devotion to God, Matthew tells this story of spontaneous and unseemly devotion.

So yes, it's totally possible to get all caught up in a freaky shopping trance and spend way outside your budget on useless stuff produced under questionable circumstances. Yes, we should all buy thoughtfully, paying attention to the way our items are made and the way that those who produce and sell them are treated. But to hear some people tell it, to see the way some people eye a full shopping bag at this time of year, you'd think that your shopping list is the final straw, the one that's going to ruin Christmas for everyone, everywhere.

So to all the lecturers out there: lighten up. You're right that Jesus would rather have you give to a good charity than buy whatever just caught your eye in the checkout line. But he'd also rather have his birthday party full of fun, generous people than grumpy, judgmental gits.

*God, fill me so full of love that it spills out into the world. Amen.*

When they saw the star, they were filled with joy. They entered the house and saw the child with Mary his mother. Falling to their knees, they honored him. Then they opened their treasure chests and presented him with gifts of gold, frankincense, and myrrh. (Matthew 2:10-11)

The nativity scene we set up in our house every year while I was growing up had all the standard bits, and then some: Mary and Joseph and the baby. An angel. A star. More animals than you can imagine, including Rudolph, Snoopy, and a random penguin.

What it didn't have were the three wise men. I'm pretty sure my mom hated them.

"Only a man," I remember her saying. "Only a man would be stupid enough to bring perfume and jewelry and spices to a new mother. She doesn't need that stuff! She doesn't need myrrh; the woman needs diapers! She needs a hotel room! She doesn't need frankincense; she needs a nap! Men," she would finish, shaking her head in disgust.

See, she'd been young and scared and poor herself once, holding a baby she didn't know what to do with. She could imagine what it had been like, and she had no patience for fools who couldn't.

However, the poor wise men had no

idea who they were going to see. Their only birth announcement was a star in the sky. So they thought they were off to visit a regular king, not a Jesus kind of king. They thought they were shopping for the baby who not only had everything but had servants to bring it to him, too. So they brought nice gifts, just not exactly appropriate ones.

If you were shopping for God, would you go to Target or Hammacher Schlemmer or Babies R Us or Tiffany's? Is the baby exalted or humble? Lord of the universe or charity case next door? And what do you get for a God who's both?

*God, I know you love any gift of a generous heart, and there's nothing you need that I can give. So I'm just going to do my best here. And I'll be sure to include a gift receipt. Amen.*

# Christmas Calendar
## WEEK THREE

**15** Put on the cheesiest Christmas album you can find. Make sure one of the songs is "The Little Drummer Boy."

**16** Now find somebody else to sing along with and do it again.

**17** Find an animal you love (in a pinch, a human will do), and spend some quality fur time together.

**18** Honor Saint Anne: call a grandmother you know (yours or someone else's) and tell her how wonderful she is.

**19** Feed someone today. Prepare the food as carefully as if you were making it to serve to God; you just might be!

**20** If you're having a sucky Christmas, hang a decoration or bake a dessert anyway. If you're having a great year, pray for someone who isn't.

**21** Light a fire tonight. A candle will do, but if you can manage a bonfire, go for it!

# December 15

"With all my heart I glorify the Lord! In the depths of who I am I rejoice in God my savior. He has looked with favor on the low status of his servant. Look! From now on, everyone will consider me highly favored because the mighty one...

... has done great things for me. Holy is his name. He shows mercy to everyone, from one generation to the next, who honors him as God. He has shown strength with his arm. He has scattered those with arrogant thoughts and proud inclinations. He has pulled the powerful down from their thrones and lifted up the lowly. He has filled the hungry with good things and sent the rich away empty-handed. He has come to the aid of his servant Israel, remembering his mercy, just as he promised to our ancestors, to Abraham and to Abraham's descendants forever." (Luke 1:46-55)

I remember my mom teaching me to sing "Silent Night." I remember my sister teaching me "O Come, All Ye Faithful." I remember how much my grandmother loved "The Little Drummer Boy," and so I love it, too, even though I think it's cheesy as Doritos.

As soon as Mary gets together with her relative Elizabeth, she starts to sing a Christmas song. We don't know where she learned it, who taught it to her, if Elizabeth knew it too, or if they had ever sung it together before. But I bet neither of them ever forgot that moment.

Who taught you the songs of this season? At whose knee, or on whose breast, did you first breath them in? Whose face appears before you whenever you hear them? Today, sing a carol or two for all the Elizabeths out there, the family members—whether by blood or otherwise—with whom you've given voice to the faith of this season. Sing for Jesus, of course, but sing for what we learned in him: the nurture of a fathering God, the strength of a mothering God, the delight of a wacky aunt or zany uncle God, the love of an adopting God.

If you're lucky enough to be able to do it, go find the person who taught you a song, or call him, and ask him to sing with you. If you can't reach her anymore, sing with her anyway, and praise God's holy name.

*God, thank you for the family that taught my soul to magnify you. Hear me as I belt your praises with them today. Amen.*

*Teach and warn each other with all wisdom by singing psalms, hymns, and spiritual songs. Sing to God with gratitude in your hearts. (Colossians 3:16)*

There are something like 5,400 animal species that make complex, intentional, repeatable, musical vocalizations. Which is to say that there are about 5,400 animal species that sing. The majority live in the trees, a few live in the oceans, a very few live underground, but there is one—only one—singing species that lives on the ground. You guessed it: us.

Humans are also the only singing species with a precise and shared sense of rhythm, which is what allows us to sing together. Two birds might sing the same song, but they can't coordinate it. They can sing next to each other but not together.

Another thing: if a roomful of people sings at the same time, they start to breathe at the same time as well. And not only that, but studies have also shown that when people sing together, their hearts start beating together, too. And if we're singing together and breathing together and our hearts are beating together, then it's like we're one body. And that's nice when you're at a

# EVENING

stadium concert or whatever and all the fans are singing along with an artist you love. But in the church, we make a bigger claim than just that we're fans vibing together; we claim that we actually become the body of the One to whom we're singing.

Most other animals stop singing when danger approaches. But humans, at least humans in Advent, sing louder the closer the danger gets. We know what stalks us, and we won't let it shut us up. We sing together and we become large and we become a Body that does not back down.

*So come at us, predators.*

*Come, Loneliness, and we will sing to you of Emanuel, God with us.*
*Come, Death, for Hark, the Herald Angels sing that Christ is*
 *risen with healing in his wings.*
*Come, Depression, and we will sing "Gloria in excelsis Deo," and*
 *we will hold that long o until you are no more.*
*Come, Power, and we will sing to you that the first Noel was to*
 *poor shepherds.*
*Come, Despair, and we will sing joy to your world.*
*Come, Racism. Come, homophobia. Come sexism. For tonight is*
 *your silent night.*
*Come, War, and we will sing you to sleep.*
*Come, all ye faithful, and sing.*

*Lord, I can't read music, and I can't carry a tune in a bucket. But I'm going to sing your praises anyway. Amen.*

# December 16

*God has exalted Jesus to his right side as leader and savior so that he could enable Israel to change its heart and life and to find forgiveness for sins. (Acts 5:31)*

I had this one poor teacher in elementary school who yelled a lot. She had a whole list of words she used to scold us: *tattletale, daydreamer, wiseacre* (which was my personal favorite even though I could never figure out what being mouthy had to do with farms). But the worst thing she could call you was *instigator.* She would jab you in the chest with a finger and spit that word at you like it tasted bad. Its use always led—at least—to you sitting in your chair, watching everybody else outside during recreation. In her mind, an instigator was the one who got all the troublemakers and bullies to ruin her life and send her to the teacher's lounge for a *lot* of furiously smoked cigarettes.

After Jesus' death and resurrection, the apostles were forever getting themselves in trouble. The line above is from Peter, saying that God has made Jesus "leader and savior," but the word here translated as "leader" also means—you guessed it—"instigator." This works for me partly because it's hilarious to think of my teacher scolding Jesus in her raspy voice, but mostly because it's true. Who sent those disciples out to say things that would whip up angry mobs? Who told them to share their faith? Who made them brave?

In time, the apostles themselves became instigators. Then their followers did, right on down to today. And now the question is, have you done enough instigating recently to make my teacher mad at you?

If not, then here's your mid-Advent assignment. Today, forget the shopping, cards, or whatever other normal Christmassy stuff you had planned. Instead, call somebody up and instigate something awesome. Get them to write letters for Amnesty International with you. Get them to go Christmas caroling to strangers' houses. Get them to make some signs that say, "War is not the answer; honk if you love the Prince of Peace!" and stand on a busy corner with you.

Jesus is on his way. It's time to raise a ruckus.

*God, grant me the grace not just to shake up the world on your behalf, but to get the people around me to do it, too. And bless Miss You-Know-Who; after all those years teaching us, she needs it. Amen.*

December 16

*All the tax collectors and sinners were gathering around Jesus to listen to him. The Pharisees and legal experts were grumbling, saying, "This man welcomes sinners and eats with them." (Luke 15:1-2)*

Communion (a.k.a. the Lord's Supper, a.k.a. the Eucharist) is one of the central rituals of the Christian faith. It celebrates and reenacts the final meal that Jesus shared with his closest friends and followers before his death.

Whenever we celebrate it at my church, the last thing I say is, "The first time Jesus sat down to this meal, among those gathered there were one who would doubt him, one who would deny him, one who would betray him, and they would all leave him alone before that night was over—and he knew it. Still he sat down and ate with them. If he ate with them, surely he's ready to eat with us—baptized or not, confessed or not, Christian or not, sure or not, believer or not, saint or sinner or a little of both. All you have to be to eat at this table is hungry. All things are ready; come, taste, and see how good God is."

A prison chaplain told me that he had "stolen" those lines (that's cool; I'm pretty sure I stole them from somebody else in the first place) and begun using them when he celebrated communion at the prison. More than once, people who had never done so before had come forward to receive communion. With tears in their eyes, they told him that they'd assumed that their crimes had made them unwelcome at the table. They'd heard others invite them but had never believed it until the chaplain reminded them who Jesus himself ate—*eats*—with.

"This fellow welcomes sinners and eats with them?" That's my only hope.

*Come, God, come. Preside at every table where I will eat today, and do not turn away the sinners, for I don't want to go hungry. Amen.*

## December 17

*Righteousness will be the belt around his hips, and faithfulness the belt around his waist. The wolf will live with the lamb, and the leopard will lie down with the young goat; the calf and the young lion will feed together, and a little child will lead them. (Isaiah 11:5-6)*

Partway into Isaiah's grand vision of what the best king ever is going to be like, the prophet abruptly switches to a description of what the world will be like when he reigns. The first thing he describes? Nature. When the world is rightly ordered, then even nature will live and thrive in peace.

On the one hand, I used to think it presumptuous to claim that the human savior (as Christians later came to understand the guy described in Isaiah's vision) was going to save everything else as well. On the other hand, no other species has the power to disrupt nature that we have, to raise the temperature on the whole planet or remove entire mountaintops. So maybe we're the only species that can save everybody else, too. Maybe the first way you know that a ruler or government or savior is ruling well is that the natural world is tended to and healthy. Maybe the first way you know that a ruler has been sent by God is that God takes care of the home as well as the people in it.

Today, spend some time considering

the rulers in your life: presidents, congresspeople, mayors, councilors, or whoever. Are their policies and their actions calibrated for the whole world or just for those who can get them reelected? Do they care about the leopards and the calves or just about the job creators? Which do you care about? How are you going to tell them?

*Lord, send us leaders wise enough to care for the creation and strong enough to save it—and make me one of them. Amen.*

*God said to Noah and to his sons with him, "I am now setting up my covenant with you, with your descendants, and with every living being with you— with the birds, with the large animals, and with all the animals of the earth, leaving the ark with you. (Genesis 9:8-10)*

Read today's passage carefully.

Did you catch that? In today's story, which comes near the end of the whole ark episode, God makes a covenant not just with Noah and his descendants, but *with every living animal, everywhere.*

How does one make a covenant with an animal? A covenant is a contract, pure and simple, an agreement between two parties that spells out how they will behave with one another. "If you give me X, I will give you Y." "If I do this, you will do that." Quid pro quo.

So what is the birds' *quid* to God's *quo*? What is it that God needs, or even wants, enough to make a contract with zebras? What could dolphins possibly do that's enough to pay for God's offer of a future? Of course, it's entirely possible that dolphins *are* doing something super important for God, and we're just too thick, or too terrestrial, to know what it is.

But really, I think that what your cat can offer God for her salvation is just what you

# EVENING

can offer: exactly nothing. It turns out that covenants with God aren't quite the same as covenants with everyone else. It turns out that with God, it's not so much a quid pro quo as a *quid pro nil*. The promise, the salvation, the future on offer to every living thing is free, and there's nothing you or your cat can do to earn it or to lose it. You might manage to get in the way of it a little, to trip it up some like a cat underfoot, but you'll never manage to stop it.

So why don't you go find an animal you know, and celebrate?

*(best said while holding or snuggling your favorite animal) God, I thank you that in you, through you, and with you, the world, the animals, and I have a future. Amen.*

## December 18

*When Elizabeth was six months pregnant, God sent the angel Gabriel to Nazareth, a city in Galilee, to a virgin who was engaged to a man named Joseph, a descendant of David's house. The virgin's name was Mary. (Luke 1:26-27)*

They say Mary's parents were named Joachim and Anne. This isn't anywhere in the Bible, but other ancient sources say so. Legend has it that they were deeply devoted to each other but were unhappy at their childlessness. Then one day, an angel appeared to each of them separately and told them—guess what?—that they were going to have a baby. A popular theme for medieval paintings was their "huggy" meeting at the gates of Jerusalem, where they had each come running from opposite directions to tell the other what had happened. Another popular one showed a wee Jesus sitting on Mary's lap, who in turn is sitting on Anne's lap.

I love St. Anne. Not so much because I know anything about her, but because I love the idea of Jesus having a grandma. I bet she was always buying him too many presents. She probably let him stay up late when he spent the weekend at her house. I bet she never told him she couldn't play right now because she was busy. I can totally see her rolling her eyes at Mary and Joseph's uptight parenting.

"Mom, stop it! You'll spoil him!" Mary would say.

"That's the Grand-Messiah's job," Anne would respond serenely as she sailed by with more cookies for the Savior.

"What am I going to do?" Mary would ask as they had coffee and watched him play. And Anne would put her arms around that big girl who would never stop being her baby, pull her close, and hold her tight. "You're going to do what we all do: love him as hard as you can. No matter what."

*God, thank you for grandparents who never stop being parents. Amen.*

December 18

*"With all my heart I glorify the Lord! In the depths of who I am I rejoice in God my savior. He has looked with favor on the low status of his servant. Look! From now on, everyone will consider me highly favored because the mighty one has done great things for me. Holy is his name. He shows mercy to everyone, from...*

*...one generation to the next, who honors him as God. He has shown strength with his arm. He has scattered those with arrogant thoughts and proud inclinations. He has pulled the powerful down from their thrones and lifted up the lowly. He has filled the hungry with good things and sent the rich away empty-handed. He has come to the aid of his servant Israel, remembering his mercy, just as he promised to our ancestors, to Abraham and to Abraham's descendants forever." (Luke 1:46-55)*

I don't know where the world got the idea that Mary was meek and mild, but wherever it was, it wasn't from a story they read in the Bible. It certainly wasn't from this passage, called the Magnificat after its first word in Latin.

First of all, she survives being an unwed teenage mother. No small feat in any age, but perhaps even harder then than now. Then, at least as the Gospel of Matthew tells it, she and her family become refugees, fleeing the murderous rage of their king, who is so terrified of the boy she's raising that he declares all the kids of his age in town to be put to death.

Never mind that she's raising the person who ended up being so important that time itself was split into "before" and "after" him. Never mind that she put up with it when he got too big for his britches and told her he didn't need her anymore. Never mind that she watched him die.

Even if all that hadn't happened, the Magnificat alone would be enough to qualify her as one hard-core mother. Picture it: in her mid-teens, pregnant, her hands resting on her growing belly, her eyes narrowed and chin up, and threatening the rich and powerful with nothing but her uterus and God's promise.

She's Rosa Parks. She's Elizabeth the First. She's Wangari Maathai. She's Joan of Arc. Or she would be, except that she's the one who formed the one who enabled all those others to do what they did.

So, who's been telling you lately that you ought to be meek and mild, and about what? And how are you going to bring them down from their thrones instead?

*God, fill me up now with your Holy Spirit, and make me a total rebel, just like Mary. Amen.*

December 19

*Since Joseph belonged to David's house and family line, he went up from the city of Nazareth in Galilee to David's city, called Bethlehem, in Judea. He went to be enrolled together with Mary, who was promised to him in marriage and who was pregnant. (Luke 2:4-5)*

Poor Joseph. He gets engaged, and then suddenly finds out he's been cuckolded—whether by another guy or by God hardly matters—and his wife's pregnant. He tries to do the right thing and leave her quietly, but then he gets bullied by an angel into doing an even righter thing. He marries and cares for Mary, adopts Jesus, and makes him his own. All this, and he barely gets a mention in the Bible. How many hymns about Joseph do you know? Would you even notice if the figure of Joseph went missing from your nativity scene? I mean, half the time you can't even remember which one is Joseph and which is the shepherd.

He deserves better, you know?

In the Middle Ages, they had a special Latin title for him: *Nutritor Domini*. It means "Feeder of the Lord." In one sense, this just meant that he was the family's provider, the one who brought home the bacon. Well, not bacon; they were Jewish. But you know what I mean.

In another sense, *Nutritor Domini* is a

much more tender and intimate title. *Nutritor* is an uncommon word; it is the male form of *nutrix*. And do you know what a *nutrix* was? A wet nurse, or one who breastfed a baby when the baby's biological mother couldn't do it herself. In calling Joseph *Nutritor Domini*, they were implying that Joseph's care was as gentle and as loving as breastfeeding. They were saying that he was the one who stood in for the Parent, the one who made Jesus eat his broccoli, argued with him about sugary cereals, gave him his goldfish crackers and juice boxes and cheese sticks. He didn't have to do it. He chose to. And then look what happened.

Today, in honor of Joseph, find a way to feed somebody who needs it. Say a kind word to a grumpy person, buy a sandwich for the guy on the street, call your lonely old uncle, write a letter to your congressperson and tell her food access for all matters to you.

When God was born into the world tiny, squalling and help-less, Joseph could have walked away. Instead, he picked the baby up, shuffled out to the kitchen in the dark, and started heating up a bottle.

*God, you show up in the most unlikely of places. Let me be wise enough and tender enough to feed you when you do. Amen.*

*This is how the birth of Jesus Christ took place. When Mary his mother was engaged to Joseph, before they were married, she became pregnant by the Holy Spirit. Joseph her husband was a righteous man. Because he didn't ...*

*... want to humiliate her, he decided to call off their engagement quietly. As he was thinking about this, an angel from the Lord appeared to him in a dream and said, "Joseph son of David, don't be afraid to take Mary as your wife, because the child she carries was conceived by the Holy Spirit. (Matthew 1:18-20)*

OK, I'm going to tell you something that maybe nobody's ever told you before: your dreams are boring. I know, I know: that superpowers dream was so amazing. I know, I know: the one with your dead grandma was so sad and the one with the monster was so scary and the one about your junior high math teacher was so… intense. I know. But seriously, *your dreams are boring to everybody except you.* Even your therapist only listens because you pay her.

Unless, that is, you're like Joseph. That guy can *dream*. Not the "Whoa you guys, I had the weirdest dream last night" kind of dream. And not the "I'm going to be president and have a million dollars one day" kind of dream, either. He dreams the way Martin Luther King Jr. dreams. He has the kind of dreams that save the world.

Joseph's dreams aren't the product of random neurons firing in his brain or his subconscious working something out. They're a glimpse into the heart of God. They're visions of the land where people believe in miracles and every baby everywhere is kept safe and tyrants don't win and you can always go home again. They make him brave, bold, gentle. They make him willing to bet everything on God's being right. They don't make him want to talk; they make him want to act.

If you have a regular dream tonight, do the world a favor and keep it to yourself tomorrow. But if you have a dream like Joseph's, you better dish.

*God, spare me the flying dreams. Make me like Joseph instead: let me see visions and dream the kind of dreams that only you can give. And tomorrow morning, let me make them real. Amen.*

# December 20

It looks like Joseph is on track to have the suckiest Christmas ever. Well, OK, Christmas didn't exactly exist just yet, but you know what I mean. He's just found out that his young fiancée cheated on him (or so it would appear), and not only that, she's pregnant with the other dude's baby. I bet he didn't send out cards that year.

I can relate. There was the year my oldest sister was gravely ill and was in and out of the hospital. There was the year the same thing happened to my middle sister, but with a different illness. There was the year half the family was in a giant feud. There was the year my father's long final illness ended a few days after Christmas.

And yet, in each of these years, we went ahead with Christmas. We always had a tree—a real one, the kind that takes a bunch of work to deal with. And I remember realizing, that year my dad was dying, that Christmas trees aren't always an expression of serene joy. They're not icing on the yummy cake. They're not gilding on the lily of a perfect life. At least sometimes, they're the only beautiful thing in the middle of a wasteland. At least sometimes, they're a giant, shiny, shimmery one-finger salute flashed in the face of a cruel world.

That year, every little glass ball I put on the tree felt like an act of defiance. As I hung each ornament, it was like I was shouting, "Take that, misery!" "Eat it, addiction!" "Bite me, cancer!" "Die, death." If you're having the suckiest Christmas ever, just remember that that's how Christmas started. It was born in defiance of all that stalks the world and tries to snuff its light. Today, decorate something whether you feel like it or not. Let each star and bow be a sucker punch in the face of what ails you. Let every candy cane be a raging against the dying of the light. Let every battered old ornament be the star that changes everything.

And if you can't manage to decorate your whole house this year, if all you can manage is one decoration hanging on a houseplant, let it be the best one you have. And tell despair it better watch its back.

*Oh God, some Christmases I just can't even. But I know you can. Come, God, come. Amen.*

December 20

*The earth dries up and wilts; the world withers and wilts; the heavens wither away with the earth. From the ends of the earth we have heard songs: "Glory to the righteous one!" (Isaiah 24:4, 16)*

It's become common for churches to hold a "Blue Christmas" service around this time of year. They're designed to be a safe and supportive place for those dealing with hard stuff made harder by Christmas, for those who aren't feeling what everybody else assumes is the proper Christmas spirit. I've held these services myself and probably will again, but I always worry about them a little.

I worry about them partly because it seems strange to me to set aside a special service for the odd ones out, as if they were losers or weirdos who needed to be quarantined from the general population. But really, I worry about them because it seems to me that every Advent service ought to be a Blue Christmas service. The Bible makes clear that the context for Christmas isn't rejoicing; it's desolation. It's not fullness; it's need. It's not presence; it's absence. If things weren't pretty messed up for everybody, why would God have bothered?

# EVENING

The time for Christmas carols isn't just when you're feeling great; the time is when you have to force them out through lips slack with depression or trembling with grief. The time for "O Come, O Come, Emmanuel" isn't just when you're convinced it's going to happen; it's when you really, really want it to happen but are mostly convinced it won't.

Look, I don't want you to spend December wallowing; if you're feeling OK, great! God's coming on your behalf, too. I just want to be sure you know that if the only spirit you can get into is low, you're just who God is looking for.

*Whether I'm happy or sad, brave or terrified, healthy or sick, or all at once, I will sing your praises. Come, God, come. Amen.*

Moses was taking care of the flock for his father-in-law Jethro, Midian's priest. He led his flock out to the edge of the desert, and he came to God's mountain called Horeb. The Lord's messenger appeared to him in a flame of fire...

*... in the middle of a bush. Moses saw that the bush was in flames, but it didn't burn up. (Exodus 3:1-2)*

Admit it: you love fire. Even though you're a little scared of it, there's a part of you that loves it, that's drawn to it like a moth to a you-know-what.

There are fireplace people. Backyard bonfire people. Campfire people. Wood-stove people. Scented tealight people. Barbeque people. Gas stovetop people, who would never dream of cooking on an electric range. And don't forget religious people throughout the world who, though we don't have to do it to survive, set fire to millions of things every week, which we call "candles."

Fire is at the heart of human experience; arguably, learning how to interact with it intentionally—to cast light and create heat—was the first truly human act. At the same time, like all animals, we have an instinctive fear of it and what it can do.

No wonder it's such a powerful symbol

for God. No wonder, too, that the fire-setting kicks into such high gear around this time of year: Advent candles on wreaths, bayberry candles in the windows, chestnuts roasting on open fires (although, seriously, has anybody ever actually done that?). And don't forget the lights on your Christmas tree, which are really just a form of safety fire that's less likely to burn the house down.

And all of it to proclaim this: Like the sun consenting to come out of the sky and warm up your living room by burning merrily in the hearth. Like a nuclear reaction reigning itself in until you can bake cookies with it. Like a blue-white star diminishing itself until it can burn at the end of your wick while you sing "Silent Night," the Creator of heaven and earth came to us one day as a human baby, who was the Light of the World.

You should set something on fire today to celebrate.

*Thank you, God, for fire. For diminishing yourself until you could show us the way without blinding us, warm us without burning us, and hold us without consuming us, thank you. Amen.*

## December 21

*Night will be no more. They won't need the light of a lamp or the light of the sun, for the Lord God will shine on them. . . . (Revelation 22:5)*

Today was the shortest day, and tonight was the longest night. The winter solstice. On the solstice, the dark beats out the light: fifteen hours of darkness per day. The earth itself has turned away from the sun. Anyone who reads the newspapers is likely to ask the question the ancients asked on this night: where is the light?

Most of the time, we light candles to remind us that God is light and that God is in the world. Most of the time, candles are enough. But on the shortest day, candles are not enough. On the longest night, the world needs a larger and a wilder light than that.

Just as, when once upon a time, the shadows grew, and the earth had turned its face away from God, it needed a larger and a wilder hope than ever before. And so God came to shine in the darkness:

To burn in the hearts of a thousand peacemakers. To set a fire of passion for healing. To set the depressed alight with the strength for one more day. To give the people hope. To set a wildfire of repentance and a longing for justice gently overwhelming the whole world. To turn the earth back to the sun.

And so God came to blaze in the hearts of the people.

And so we come, to light bonfires of love in the desert. And so we come, to tell the world that the night will not win. And so we come, we who seek to follow the light, to shine the light on the world.

Tonight, do what the ancients did on the solstice: light a fire. Make it the biggest one you can. If a candle in a dark room is the best you can manage, fine. If you have the space for a gasoline-accelerated bonfire in the backyard, go for it. Remind the world—remind *yourself*—that the shadows will not win.

*Come, God, come, and shine. Amen.*

# Christmas Calendar
## WEEK FOUR

**22** Adopt someone today: invite a new person over for a family tradition. Treat her like a member of the family (or better).

**23** If you're a churchgoer, make plans with someone to go to church with you tomorrow night. If you're not, then get someone to take you!

**24** Go to a Christmas Eve service. Pause in the dark outside after the service. Breathe.

**25** Delight in bodily pleasures today. Dedicate them to God.

**26** Make plans to return that one present (you know the one). Reflect on what you really want.

**27** Make love today. Make it generous, gentle, and delightful. You deserve it!

**28** Pray for children living with violence. Do a little research online about how you can help end the violence.

# December 22

Ask the average person what the most boring part of the Bible is, and ten to one they'll say, "The begats." By which they'll mean the genealogies that show up here and there, including here at the beginning of Matthew's telling of Jesus' story.

But family histories are important, and if you look deeply enough into this one of Matthew's, you'll find nestled in the great long lists of names (which you'll suspect somebody just had to have made up as filler) some truly juicy bits and some truly awesome skeletons hidden away. There's Jacob, who tricked his brother out of the family inheritance and ran away with it. There's Tamar, who pretended to be a prostitute in order to sleep with her father-in-law and become pregnant with the sons that her husbands hadn't given her. There's Rahab, a foreign woman who betrayed her own people for the Israelites. There's Ruth, another foreigner, who took her family's fate into her own hands to save them. There's David, who had a child with Bathsheba after having her husband killed so he could get with her. Incest, murder, prostitution, betrayal, thievery, all manner of pregnancies out of wedlock.

And you thought your family was messed up.

Jesus wasn't born into some unsullied house, perfect of pedigree and noble of history. He was born into a human family, one at least as complicated as yours, just as full of rifts, betrayals, and shameful secrets.

If God can pull salvation out of that family, then surely God can do the same for yours. No matter what your great uncle Larry did.

*God, if you can make a child of that family the savior of the world, then surely there's hope for this child, too. Thanks for not letting my beginnings be my destiny. Amen.*

Jacob was the father of Joseph, the husband of Mary—of whom Jesus was born, who is called the Christ. (Matthew 1:16)

Here's a weird thing about the Bible: it traces Jesus' lineage through Joseph, not Mary.

But I thought Jesus was *God* and Mary's son, not *Joseph* and Mary's son! I mean, the Bible goes to all kinds of trouble to make sure you know that Joseph did not contribute to Jesus' conception. So why is Matthew tracing Jesus' genealogy through Joseph?

One word: adoption.

Every once in a while, I'll hear somebody say something derogatory about adopted kids versus biological kids. My husband and I are adoptive fathers ourselves, and so hearing these kinds of comments makes me want to punch the speaker in the throat—or it would if I weren't committed to nonviolent responses to stupidity.

So instead, I'll often point out that the Messiah, the Prince of Peace, was an adopted kid and that Joseph's adoption of him made him so fully a part of the family that the Bible itself doesn't have a moment's hesitation in naming him the heir of King David.

# EVENING

This, I believe, is no accident. The story of the people of our God is the story of adoption. It's the story of a God who makes a way where there is no way, who makes a people where there is no people. It's the story of a God who was once born into the world needing to be adopted himself and who found a great forever family. A God who says over and over and over, "This family is nuts, but if you want in, we'll take you." Who will never leave the foreigner, the widow, the orphan, or you, without a family if you want one.

What families have adopted you? What group, or maybe just one person, has taken you in and treated you like blood? What you ought to do is call them up and tell them they acted as God to you. But since that would probably be too weird, why not just say "Thanks"?

*God, for adopting me into this family, and for making it mine, thank you. Amen.*

*The* Lord *said to Moses, "Go and leave this place, you and the people whom you brought up out of the land of Egypt. Go to the land I promised to Abraham, Isaac, and Jacob when I said, 'I'll give it to your descendants.' Go to this land …*

*…full of milk and honey. But I won't go up with you because I would end up destroying you along the way since you are a stubborn people." (Exodus 33:1, 3)*

"W hy don't you guys go out back?" my mother would say to us kids. "You could turn on the hose/swing on the rope/play lawn darts*/build a fort!" She would say it like it was an option. But the astute observer (and we learned to be, fast) would notice a certain manic gleam in her eye and the fact that she was speaking through clenched teeth, suggesting an unspoken ending to the invitation: "Because if you don't get out of this house *right now*, somebody's going to get it."

That's the mood God's in here. Moses has just come down off the mountain and caught the people worshiping a golden idol. So God says through clenched teeth, "Why don't you guys head over that way—*right now*." And God doesn't leave the rest unspoken: "Because if you kids don't get out of my sight *this instant*, I will consume you."

Jeez. Even my mom at her scariest never threatened to consume us.

Eventually, my mom would call us in for dinner, and all would be cool. Well, unless we ignored her long enough to make her say something like, "Don't make me come out there and get you!" Then we were sort of back where we started. But you get the point.

Christmas Eve is tomorrow, and if you're like the rest of us, it's one of those times that you can hear the call to come back inside a little more clearly. Maybe you were kicked out back once upon a time. Maybe you stormed out. Maybe you just sort of wandered out.

If you're not sure where to go, get a friend or family member you trust to take you to their church. Or come up with search terms that would describe your dream church, and Google them along with the name of your town.

You might as well go on back inside. It's getting cold out, and chances are, there will be dessert.

*Yes, I'm serious. You can't make this stuff up.

*God, I know I get on your nerves sometimes. But you get on mine, too. Thanks for loving me anyway. Amen.*

A shoot will grow up from the stump of Jesse;
a branch will sprout from his roots. (Isaiah 11:1)

In the 1930s, a young woman named Marjorie Courtenay-Latimer was working as a museum official in South Africa. She had spread the word around that she was interested in seeing any interesting specimens anybody turned up, and on the twenty-third of December 1938, she got a call. Some local fishermen had brought in a very strange fish indeed. She had no idea what the huge, bluish-purple fish with hard scales and four limblike fins was, but she knew it was special.

It took quite a while for the experts to positively identify it, but they eventually confirmed that it was a coelacanth, an ancient species that until then people thought had been extinct for sixty-five million years. Since then, specimens have been found up and down the eastern coast of Africa. They call it a "living fossil" because living specimens look pretty much just like the ones in the fossil record. But I don't think that name's fair. That implies that it's primarily just a dead thing preserved in rock, instead of a living thing that's been tough enough to survive in sixty-five million years' worth of changing conditions. Instead of calling it a "living fossil," why not just call it "living"?

Back in Isaiah's day, lots of people thought the tree of Jesse, God's chosen line of leaders and saviors, had been cut down forever. They thought the promises of God had ended, that the species had gone extinct. Some, like Isaiah, believed that it would come back, would be rediscovered someplace unexpected. For most, the tree of Jesse and the hope it bore was just part of the fossil record.

And then, suddenly, there it was again, sprouting up in the desert, tough enough to have survived a lot of years' worth of changing conditions. A young woman named Mary discovered it first, growing in her womb. It took quite a while for the experts to positively identify it, because unlike the coelacanth, it looked a little different than it used to. Marjorie Courtenay-Latimer would have said that its morphology had evolved. I'll just say that Jesus wasn't quite what anybody expected. He might have looked different than people were expecting, but he was the same line, the same promise, the same hope, the same species as all God's promises. Not a "living fossil"—just living.

*God, for promises that last for generations, thank you. Amen.*

Nearby shepherds were living in the fields, guarding their sheep at night. The Lord's angel stood before them, the Lord's glory shone around them, and they were terrified. The angel said, "Don't be afraid! Look! I bring good news to you—

...wonderful, joyous news for all people. Your savior is born today in David's city. He is Christ the Lord. This is a sign for you: you will find a newborn baby wrapped snugly and lying in a manger." Suddenly a great assembly of the heavenly forces was with the angel praising God. They said, "Glory to God in heaven, and on earth peace among those whom he favors." (Luke 2:8-14)

Introverts and loners take note: news of the saving of the world came to you first. People who aren't that good at being around other people, look up: the angels came to you, not to the highly social or well connected. Those who prefer the company of animals to that of humans, good news: God thought you ought to be the first to know.

Shepherds in Jesus' day weren't known for their gregariousness or for the extent of their social networks. They spent days, weeks at a time with no company but their flocks and their predators. When they came back from the range or down from the hills,

they were known for their awkwardness, even standoffishness.
I assume they didn't show up at worship that often.

And yet, when they heard what had happened, they went
running to find the baby and his parents. And not only that, they
told everyone they met what had happened. They didn't hide
out in their comfortable solitude; they went right to the center
of the action. Sooner or later they had to go back to the fields,
but it's hard to imagine they were quite the same when they
went back as they had been when they came.

So I get that you might be a loner. I get that you may not be
a fan of other people or organized religion. I get that you prefer
your own private spirituality and would rather stay home with a
book than be with a bunch of strangers. But the Christmas story
calls us, I think, into contact with other people. It demands that
we gather once in a while. It invites us to engage.

So, no loner-ing allowed this evening. Tonight, get your butt
to church.

*OK, God, I'm willing to go. But I'm totally going to hide out in my*
*room for a week after that, and you can't stop me. Amen.*

## December 24

"Look! I bring good news to you—wonderful, joyous news for all people. Your savior is born today in David's city. He is Christ the Lord." (Luke 2:10-11)

Here's what I say at the beginning of every Christmas Eve service, right after welcoming everybody:

*"If you came to this place expecting a tame story, you came to the wrong place.*

*If you came for a story that does not
       threaten you,
you came for a different story than the one
       we tell.*

*If you came to hear of the coming of a God
who only showed up so that you could have a
       nice day
with your loved ones,
then you came for a God whom we do not
       worship here.*

*For even a regular baby is not a tame thing.
And goodness that cannot threaten compla-
       cency and evil
is not much good at all,
And a God who would choose to give up power
       and invincibility*

# EVENING

to become an infant for you,
certainly didn't do it just so you could have dinner.

But.

If you came because you think that unwed teenage mothers
are some of the strongest people in the world.

If you came because you think that the kind of people who work third
shift doing stuff you'd rather not do might attract an angel's
attention before you, snoring comfortably in your bed, would.

If you came because you think there are wise men and women to be
found among undocumented travelers from far lands and
that they might be able to show you God.

If you came to hear a story of tyrants trembling
while heaven comes to peasants.

If you came because you believe that God loves the animals
as much as the people
and so made them the first witnesses to the saving of the world.

If you came for a story of reversals
that might end up reversing you.

If you came for a tale of adventure and bravery,
where strong and gentle people win,
and the powerful and violent go down to dust,
where the rich lose their money but find their lives
and the poor are raised up like kings.

If you came to be reminded that God loves you too much
to leave you unchanged.

If you came to follow the light
even if it blinds you.

If you came for salvation and not safety,
then, ah, my friends,
you are in precisely the right place."

So what are *you* here for?

God, let this story sink so deep into me that I go to bed tonight
not sleepy and comfortable but shaken, terrified, exhilarated, and
alive. Amen.

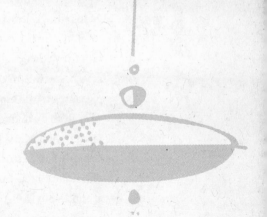

## December 25

*In the beginning was the Word and the Word was with God and the Word was God. The Word became flesh and made his home among us. (John 1:1, 14)*

This is what we celebrate: that God, who didn't need one, got a body. That God was so hungry to be close to us that nothing—not eternity, not power, not immortality—was too much to give up; and nothing—not time, not weakness, not a mortal body—was too much to take on. This is what we celebrate: God with a body.

So it's fitting that so many of our Christmas traditions have to do with delights of the flesh: eating, drinking, singing, hugging and kissing, seeing gorgeous things, hearing beautiful sounds, and smelling good smells. Each is an opportunity for worship and praise. So today of all days, take time to consecrate your fleshly pleasures to the God who consecrated your flesh by taking it on. Make them sacraments: Marvel at the miracle of food and drink. Be astounded by the sanctity of human touch. Wonder at the beauty around you. Delight in making and hearing sounds of praise. Bask in a delicious smell.

Make love to the person you truly treasure. Celebrate with your body, and say that God is great.

On Christmas, this is what we celebrate: that bodies are good, that flesh is a gift, and that our God put them both on for us. Be sure you take some time to use yours to praise God today.

*Holy and eternal one, the wonders of your love are beyond my ability to comprehend. But I thank you for my body, I thank you for getting your body, and I praise your holy name. Merry Christmas, God. Amen.*

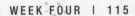

**December 25**

*The light shines in the darkness, and the darkness doesn't extinguish the light. (John 1:5)*

Now would be a good time to wrap up warm and comfy, get a drink of something good, put on some good music, turn off all the lights, pull a chair up to the window, and look.

For a prayer tonight, all you need is your own breath and no words from me. Well, maybe just three:

*Thank you. Amen.*

# EVENING

## December 26

*How long will you forget me, LORD? Forever? How long will you hide your face from me? How long will I be left to my own wits, agony filling my heart? Daily? How long will my enemy keep defeating me? (Psalm 13:1-2)*

So? Did you get everything you want? Is there a check mark next to everything on your list? And are you totally fulfilled? Completely happy?

Now let me ask a more important question: did you get everything you *truly* want? Not the stuff on the list you e-mailed to your aunt and uncle. I mean the stuff you want so bad it's more like a need. Did your disease get cured? Did your dead spouse come back? Did you and your estranged brother finally work it out? Did your depression let you get out of bed and mean it?

I really hope your answer's yes, but I fear it won't be. The commercials would have you believe Christmas is all about fulfillment: the gleam in her eyes when she opens the diamond necklace. And if at the end of Christmas, you don't feel completely fulfilled, it can seem like something went wrong.

Sometimes the church does the same thing. We make it sound like all we're waiting for in Advent is the baby, and since

God's promised to give him to us, just like a parent promising an Xbox, we'll be all set once Christmas morning comes.

But Advent isn't just about fulfillment. Advent is always about longing, and it's always about longing that's not going to be fulfilled for a long time. Christmas didn't fix everything; it *started* fixing everything. Meanwhile, we continue to wait, with all the biggest items on our lists unchecked.

And yet, after Christmas, after the baby, the tenor of our wait is different. Now, we're not waiting alone. Now, we're waiting with the God who could have remained above it all but chose to dive into it with us and not leave us until the end.

*God, I didn't get everything I wanted this year; you know I'm still waiting for some of the big-ticket items. Thanks for staying to hold my hand while I wait. Amen.*

December 26

*...Falling to his knees, he shouted, "Lord, don't hold this sin against them!" Then he died. (Acts 7:57-60)*

*Together, they charged at him, threw him out of the city, and began to stone him. The witnesses placed their coats in the care of a young man named Saul. As they battered him with stones, Stephen prayed, "Lord Jesus, accept my life!" ...*

Today is the Feast of Saint Stephen, whom history calls the first Christian martyr, stoned to death by the religious authorities.

It's also the day when, if you believe the song, good King Wenceslas looked out and saw a poverty-stricken man gathering wood against the bitter cold. The king decided to bring food and fuel to the poor man and called his young servant to help. Page and monarch went forth, but before long, the young page began to languish in the cold and came close to dying. Wenceslas told the boy to step in his footsteps, and warmth radiated up through them to save his life.

Cheesy, I know. But you guys, there's actually something to this whole giving and helping thing. *Warm* may be an overused word to describe the feelings you get when you help out, but there's a reason so many people describe it that way.

You may not have gotten all you want—you may not have gotten all you *deserve*—this Christmas. You may be staggering under the weight of what you're carrying, about to drop in the cold. But the paradox that generation upon generation of Christians has discovered, from Jesus through Wenceslas right up to today, is that the more you manage to give, the more you'll receive, and the more you pour yourself out for the poor and vulnerable, the more you find yourself filled up and, well, warmed.

So for once in your life, take a look out the window. See who's struggling past out there. And then whether you're a lowly page or a magnificent monarch, forth you go.

*O my master, let me tread in your steps, to be and to find blessing. Amen.*

*Look at how good and pleasing it is when families live together as one! It is like expensive oil poured over the head, running down onto the beard— Aaron's beard!—which extended over the collar of his robes. (Psalm 133:1-2)*

Staying with family for the holidays? Have relatives staying with you? Been to one too many gatherings with Aunt Janice?

"Look at how good and pleasant it is when families live together as one!" might be a good one to write out and tape to the bathroom mirror right about now. Or to chant on your way up the walk to your third gift exchange in as many days. Or to just whisper to yourself as you hide in the dark of the hall closet, hugging your knees and rocking back and forth in the shoe pile.

Even for those of us with kin we like, all the family togetherness this time of year can get to be a bit much. For those with more complicated dynamics in their family trees, it can be downright harrowing.

If this describes you, you're not alone. Hardly anybody gets along with their families in the Bible; and what they do to one another in there is, I promise you, way worse than your cousin's constant micro-aggressions. Jesus isn't as bad as some, but even he plays the ungrateful child, running away, telling his parents off, dismissing them and his brothers like beggars. But the promise of the Bible, the point of this whole faith thing, is that God is working in every one of them whether we can see it or not (even Aunt Janice).

The holidays won't last forever. And whether you're thrilled to be home or counting down the days till the infestation leaves your house, take heart: before this is all over, God's going to gather the whole human tribe together and somehow—somehow—make that family reunion a delight.

*God, you know how hard this can be. So help me bite my tongue when I should, act twice as lovingly as I feel, and make this family party as good and pleasant as I can. And until you perfect us all, make us kind. Amen.*

*God sent the angel Gabriel to Nazareth, a city in Galilee, to a virgin who was engaged to a man named Joseph, a descendant of David's house. The virgin's name was Mary. When the angel came to her, he said, "Rejoice, favored one! The Lord is with you! ... Don't be afraid, Mary. God is honoring you. Look! You will conceive ...*

*...and give birth to a son, and you will name him Jesus. He will be great and he will be called the Son of the Most High...and there will be no end to his kingdom." Then Mary said to the angel, "How will this happen since I haven't had sexual relations with a man?" The angel replied, "The Holy Spirit will come over you and the power of the Most High will overshadow you." (Luke 1:26-35)*

Here's what I hope for Mary: that she had a really amazing sex life.

I mean it. I know you think I'm just saying that to get a reaction out of you, but I'm serious. And let's be clear here that I'm by no means the only one talking about it. The church has been nosing its way into Mary's bedroom for years, speculating on what she was doing in there. And of course, for generation upon generation, the assumption, tellingly insisted on most loudly by the men, is that she wasn't doing anything. Knitting, perhaps. Praying. Maybe a little scrapbooking.

How would you feel about being the one for whom they coined the term *perpetual virginity*? The point here isn't about whether she was a virgin when she conceived Jesus. The point is all those years that came afterward. She became a refugee in Egypt trying to protect her son. He ran away when he was twelve. He grew up to become an itinerant preacher, and at one point he told her that she meant less to him than his disciples. She watched him die. She went through all that, and the world wants to deny her the pleasure and consolation of sex, too? I for one don't think you get to be Queen of Heaven by letting people push you around—even grumpy, uptight clergymen living generations after you.

So here's what I hope for Mary: that in the midst of all she had to do and all she had to suffer, she knew the delights of the flesh. That she learned the ways sexual love can be holy, and that she never learned the ways it can be twisted into something else. I hope that Joseph was a generous lover. I hope she knew she was pure and holy in part because of their lovemaking, not in spite of it. I hope they had a lot of fun because they sure earned it.

That's what I hope for her. Here's what I hope for you: the same thing.

*God, help me make all that I do a prayer of delight and thanksgiving to you, the one who did not disdain to get a body like ours. Amen.*

**December 28**

*When Herod knew the magi had fooled him, he grew very angry. He sent soldiers to kill all the male children in Bethlehem and in all the surrounding territory who were two years old and younger, according to the time that he had learned ...*

*...from the magi. This fulfilled the word spoken through Jeremiah the prophet:*

*A voice was heard in Ramah,*
  *weeping and much grieving.*
    *Rachel weeping for her children,*
      *and she did not want to be comforted,*
        *because they were no more.*
*(Matthew 2:16-18)*

There's nothing so terrible, they say, as the death of one's own child. It's so horrifying, so disordered that we don't even have a name for those it's happened to. People who have lost their spouses are widows or widowers; people who have lost their parents are orphans. But for those who've lost a child, we have no name. We fall silent in the face of tragedy of that magnitude.

The story above is usually called the Massacre of the Innocents. December 28 (December 29 in some places) is often called the Feast of the Holy Innocents. It's a remembrance of those who died because of others' scheming, and it's a promise to make sure never to let it happen again.

But it's also an opportunity for parents who have lost a child—not just to violence but also to miscarriage, illness, or accident—to bring the hole inside them and lay it bare before the God who is in the same nameless category as they are. Because while Jesus may have escaped the Massacre of the Innocents when he was little, death came for him eventually, too. God knows what it is to lose a child just as surely as Rachel does. Nothing this side of heaven is going to take away the pain for those whose children have died, but at least we have a God who knows what it's like.

It's not enough. But it's something.

*God, you could have saved yourself from all this. You could have stayed far above a world where things like this happens, but you didn't. Thank you. Amen.*

*Jesus' mother and his mother's sister, Mary the wife of Clopas, and Mary Magdalene stood near the cross. (John 19:25)*

They call her Queen of Heaven. She earned it.

She's the only one.

She's the only one who was there at both the beginning and the end. Joseph wasn't. Peter wasn't. Judas wasn't. The shepherds and the wise men and the animals weren't.

Not Caesar, Pilate, Caiaphas, the Centurion, the thieves, or the crowds. She was the only one who was there for his first breath and his last. The only one who went all the way with him.

Do you think she knew? Do you think she knew when she cried out in labor what other cries she would cry? When she wrapped him in bands of cloth, do you think she knew she would tie his winding sheet as well?

When she held him in her arms on that first silent night, do you think she could see the day when she would hold him in her arms on another one? And if she did, why did she do it? Why didn't she say no to that angel? Why didn't she convert to some other religion and never breathe the name of God in her son's presence?

Didn't she know what it would be like to hold her son's broken body in her arms? Hadn't she seen it so many times, to so many other women? Hadn't she seen it when the Roman legions came through and sacked their town? Hadn't she watched the local boys run off to the hills to join rebellion after doomed rebellion? Hadn't she seen enough mothers holding enough dead sons to know?

Or was that the point?

Don't you think she looked down through the years and around the globe and saw the mothers of all those hundreds of thousands kidnapped and murdered by their own governments in Central and South America, saw the mothers of the disappeared in Argentina and Chile and Colombia and Guatemala? Don't you think she knew they would need strength to put their white shawls on and go marching to stand up, to organize, to say, "No more"? Don't you think she looked down through the years and across the ocean and saw all those mothers lose their sons to slavery, to lynching, to dogs and fire hoses? Do you think she knew they would need hope to get through the day and strength for the fight?

Don't you think she saw the mothers of suicide bombers in Afghanistan who lost their boys to madness? And the mothers of every land who lost their boys to soldierhood, and to death?

Don't you think she saw the mothers in inner cities losing their boys to drugs and to gangs?

Do you think she saw all those mothers and all those broken hearts and knew that they would need to be fed with the milk of hope and strength? And do you think that's why she did what she did, even though while he was still at her breast, she could see him hanging on a tree?

Of course it is.

*For the strength of mothers in every time and place, O God, thank you. And when you see the Queen of Heaven, please tell her "Ave, Maria" from me. Amen.*

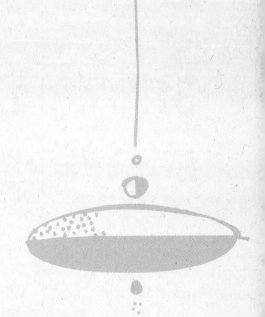

# Christmas Calendar
## WEEK FIVE

**29** Pay attention to babies today. If you can get your hands on one without upsetting anybody, hold her and delight in her: smell the top of her head, boop her nose, be amazed at those little fingers. Praise the God who showed up as one of these.

**30** Sometime today when you have a bunch of people around you, pause and check each one out (but don't be creepy). Wonder if God is coming to you in that person. Pray for him.

**31** Ask yourself: if the thing that has you held in chains was going to be abolished tonight, what would you do? Then make plans to do it!

**1** Sometime today, pick a person you're in a room with (bonus points if you pick somebody you dislike). Imagine what she'll look like shining like the sun when she gets to heaven. All day, treat her as if she's already shining.

**2** Go through your pile of Christmas cards. Pray for three people in the pile.

**3** Write down your favorite name for Jesus as beautifully as you can (use glitter if you've got it). Put it someplace you'll see it all day long.

**4** Watch a good movie about a cosmic battle between good and evil today. After Frodo's done destroying Sauron or Harry Potter scrubs Voldemort, remind yourself that the life of faith doesn't work that way.

## December 29

At that time Jesus came from Galilee to the Jordan River so that John would baptize him. When Jesus was baptized, he immediately came up out of the water. Heaven was opened to him, and he saw the Spirit of God coming down like a dove and resting on him. …

*… A voice from heaven said, "This is my Son whom I dearly love; I find happiness in him."* (Matthew 3:13, 16-17)

For most of my life, I have not been a fan of babies. I do not mean that I disliked them. I mean that my appreciation for them was academic. If someone said, "Do you want to hold the baby?" I would say, "Yes!" because I'm not stupid. But really, babies were like tigers or panoramic views: best appreciated from a distance.

Then we got one of our own, and now I'm *crazy* for them. If I see one, I long to hold her and smell her head. On the street, I make silly faces at them instead of wishing their parents would get the stroller out of my way. I frequently have to remind myself that it's rude to nibble on strangers' wee toes.

It's like our kid is a little prism that refracts my love for him out to all babies everywhere; or maybe it's that he gathers in all the babyness in the world and focuses it on my hard heart to crack it open. Babies in general couldn't do it; it took being responsible for one baby in particular to make me crazy for all of them.

Don't you think God's like that? Don't you think God loved babies in a new way after that night in Bethlehem? That when God bathed God's own son that day at the Jordan, God learned to bathe the rest of us, too? And when Jesus died, don't you think that God's heart broke, that God learned what every parent who's ever lost a child felt, and that's why God decided to defeat death forever?

Don't you think that sometimes it takes a baby to teach a father how to love?

*Thank you, God, for babies, for cracked-open hearts, and for all this love. Amen.*

*The angel said, "Don't be afraid, Zechariah. Your prayers have been heard. Your wife Elizabeth will give birth to your son and you must name him John." (Luke 1:13)*

Much is made of motherhood around Christmas, as well it should be. But too often, Joseph recedes into the background, and Zechariah, who, like Mary, receives the annunciation of his special kid's birth, hardly gets mentioned at all. So I always try to remind myself to think about the dads in this story. Those of us with good fathers, even flawed good fathers, know how important good fathering is. Those of us without good fathers know the same thing but have learned it in a much harder way.

I sometimes hear from people that they cannot refer to God as Father; they've experienced things with their human fathers that will not let them believe that a good God could be anything like them. So don't you think Joseph must have been a great dad? I mean, Jesus referred to God as Father more frequently than almost anything else, even going so far as to call God "Abba" as he was dying. Don't you think Joseph must have been really extraordinary for that metaphor to work for Jesus? Don't you think Zechariah must have been something special to raise a kid like John? Don't you think the world needs as many good fathers in it as it can get?

Maybe you ought to get in touch with a good Abba you know today—yours or somebody else's—and thank him for it.

*God, for every good dad you have sent into the world to shape and nurture it, we praise your name. Amen.*

**December 30**

*When Moses finished speaking with them, he put a veil over his face. (Exodus 34:33)*

Only a few uber-holy people ever get to see God face to face. Moses, of course, was one of them. Tradition has it that if any of the rest of us were to be confronted by God's holiness, we would be utterly destroyed. Our heads would explode. Even Moses didn't escape unscathed; God's holiness rubbed off on him, making his face glow so much that he had to wear a veil in order to keep from freaking people out.

When you think about it, the whole humans-can't-see-God-without-being-destroyed thing is actually a good explanation for Jesus: God loves us enough to want to be near us, but that would kill us. The solution? Become one of us. As the carol puts it, "Veiled in flesh the Godhead see / So your head doesn't explode . . . Hark! The herald angels sing . . ."

Or something like that. The point is that God apparently needs to veil God's holiness in order to get as close to us as God wants to. One of the veils God uses to do that is humanity itself, first in Jesus, and now also in the people who love and follow God.

Which means you should be asking yourself this: in whom has God come to me recently? My kid? That lady in line at the store? The one I love? My boss?

And what was God trying to say?

*God, when you come close to me by veiling yourself in the people around me, give me the grace to see and hear you there. Amen.*

## December 30

*...David and the entire house of Israel celebrated in the Lord's presence with all their strength, with songs, zithers, harps, tambourines, rattles, and cymbals.*
*(2 Samuel 6:3, 5)*

*They loaded God's chest on a new cart and carried it from Abinadab's house, which was on the hill. Uzzah and Ahio, Abinadab's sons, were driving the new cart. Meanwhile, ...*

A few miles west of Jerusalem is a town called Abu Ghosh. Tradition says it's the location of Abinadab's house, where the Ark of the Covenant rested before coming to Jerusalem. You might remember that the Ark was the chest—now lost—that contained the Ten Commandments.

On the highest point in Abu Ghosh, on the place where Abinadab's house is supposed to have stood, is a church called Notre Dame de l'Arche d'Alliance. In English, that's Our Lady, Ark of the Covenant.

The original Ark of the Covenant bore inside itself the terms of God's relationship with the people. That, claimed the ancient Christians, is exactly what Mary did in carrying Jesus, and so, in a splendid leap of Christian imagination, they gave her the same title.

But these days neither Ark is around anymore, and so the world needs a new one: you. It's your turn to bear the terms of God's relationship with the people—devotion, gentleness, honesty, self-control, respect, love—to the world. Nobody else is going to if you don't, and God knows the world needs it.

If it seems like too grand a task, if it sounds altogether too presumptuous to refer to yourself as the Ark of the Covenant, remember this: that's just what Mary would have said.

*God, you call me to tasks too big for me and too magnificent for me to have thought of on my own. Here am I, the servant of the Lord; let it be with me according to your word. Amen.*

# December 31

*However, we do see the one who was made lower in order than the angels for a little while—it's Jesus! He's the one who is now crowned with glory and honor . . . (Hebrews 2:9)*

Even the fanciest of human-made crowns can't compete with the one Jesus wears. To get a sense of it, climb a mountain high above the clouds, stand with a low sun at your back, and look down into the cloud layer. If you're lucky, you'll see your shadow wearing a crown like the one they say Jesus has.

This rarely experienced optical phenomenon is called—you guessed it—a glory. Google it now; it's pretty cool. No one quite understands how it happens, though we know it has to do with sunlight being bent and scattered back at the viewer.

What you have to scale a mountain in a rainstorm to maybe see, Jesus wears all the time because he scaled a cross in a firestorm. When he did it, it changed everything. The author of Hebrews claims that because of what Jesus gave up and what he refused to give up, because of what he let go of and refused to let go of, because of what he sacrificed and because of what he refused to sacrifice, the whole universe bent around him forever. His gravitational pull is now so strong that there is nothing in this world or the next, not even light itself, that can encounter him without being reflected, refracted, or rerouted into a new and more beautiful course.

You could hurtle straight into next year at the speed of light, just as you did this year, just the way you usually do. But you could also do this: become glory-fied. How might you let your life become part of the beauty that crowns that kid in the manger? How could you let your course be bent, slowed, refracted into something more beautiful than you could ever have managed on your own?

*God, I don't need to be Jesus's hat. But I sure would like to have him bend my life like that light and send it off in a new direction, shining like glory. Amen.*

*Then I saw a new heaven and a new earth, for the former heaven and the former earth had passed away, and the sea was no more.*
*(Revelation 21:1)*

The first recorded Watch Night service, which is just another name for a church service on New Year's Eve, was held by Moravians in Germany in 1732. From there, the practice spread and grew until lots of people and traditions were holding them. But the practice is nowhere more beloved than among African Americans, who remember the long, long wait for New Year's Eve 1862, when it's said that they gathered in churches throughout the land and especially in the South. They were longing for the new year harder than anyone had ever longed for it before, hoping for confirmation that on January 1, 1863, the promised enactment of the Emancipation Proclamation had taken place.

You've probably already made whatever plans you're going to make for New Year's Eve tonight. But before you put on your sparkly dress, let me ask you this: if you'd heard that you were going to be set free tomorrow, how would your celebration change? If you had gotten word that whatever it is that holds you in chains—addiction, fear, your past, a bad relationship, poverty—was about to be abolished forever, what would you do differently?

Would you go to church instead of partying? Would you go to church *and* party? Would you take off the sweatpants you were going to wear to watch the ball drop, put on a tuxedo instead, and go out dancing? Would you skip that event you didn't want to go to anyway, call someone you really love, and spend a quiet evening together? Would you pray?

Whatever changes happen for you tomorrow morning probably aren't going to be as momentous as the abolition of slavery. But why not act like they will be?

*God, stay with me while I watch this night, and teach me to expect freedom. Make me expect a whole new world. Amen.*

# January 1

*Then I saw a new heaven and a new earth, for the former heaven and the former earth had passed away, and the sea was no more. Then the one seated on the throne said, "Look! I'm making all things new." He also said, "Write this down, for these words are trustworthy and true." (Revelation 21:1, 5)*

Do you, or do you not, believe what the author of Revelation says: that God is making all things new?

Do you believe that God is working—right now—to bring this world to its fulfillment, or don't you? Look out your window. Do you believe that God is—right now—in the process of perfecting all that, or don't you? Look down at yourself. Do you, or don't you, believe that God is—right now—perfecting the very self you're looking at?

If not, fine. You're certainly not alone, and there's probably not much harm in living this year the same as you lived last year.

But if you do believe that a new world is coming to pass, then you have your work—and your hope—cut out for you in the new year. It means it's time to start practicing living like you've been made new, as if God has dressed your soul for a wedding. Like God is living next door. Like every person you meet is being molded for glory and is just a split second from shining like the sun.

Start now. Pick one thing in the room,

and imagine what that thing will be like when God's done with it. Pick one person, and imagine that God is—right now—about to reveal the glory of heaven in her; treat her that way all day long. Tomorrow, pick another, and the next day, another, and just see if a new world doesn't emerge.

*Come, God, come. Make your vision real in me. Amen.*

# January 1

*When eight days had passed, Jesus' parents circumcised him and gave him the name Jesus. This was the name given to him by the angel before he was conceived. (Luke 2:21)*

Today is the Feast of the Circumcision of Jesus, when churches around the world and down through the ages celebrate the moment of Jesus' dedication by his parents. Jewish law prescribed that boys be circumcised and dedicated eight days after their birth, so we celebrate the Feast of the Circumcision here, on the eighth day.

This was the moment when Mary and Joseph gave their son back to God. They affirmed that Jesus belonged to God before he belonged to them. They promised that they would work hard to raise him surrounded by the knowledge and the love of the Lord.

Many traditions no longer celebrate the Feast of the Circumcision. Partly this is because circumcision has always been, and continues to be, controversial for Christians. Partly this is because some of the devotional practices got pretty weird—guess what relic of Jesus' circumcision certain churches claimed to be in possession of (*shudder*).

But really, it's the thought that counts.

# EVENING

Even if you don't celebrate the physical act that goes along with it, you can still celebrate the spirit of the thing: parents so delighted by the gift they've received, so overwhelmed by gratitude, that they give that gift right back to God.

What have you received that you want to return to God? What gifts has God given you that you want to dedicate to God's service? Your money? Your incredible singing voice? Your free time? Your devastating wit? Your good looks? Your kids? Your whole life?

Whatever it is, you don't have to circumcise it; just put it to work.

*God, all that I have comes from you. Show me how to use it. Amen.*

*A man named Simeon was in Jerusalem. He was righteous and devout. He eagerly anticipated the restoration of Israel, and the Holy Spirit rested on him. The Holy Spirit revealed to him that he wouldn't die before he had seen...*

*... the Lord's Christ. Simeon took Jesus in his arms and praised God. There was also a prophet, Anna the daughter of Phanuel, who belonged to the tribe of Asher. She was very old. After she married, she lived with her husband for seven years. She was now an 84-year-old widow. She never left the temple area but worshipped God with fasting and prayer night and day. She approached at that very moment and began to praise God and to speak about Jesus to everyone who was looking forward to the redemption of Jerusalem. (Luke 2:25-26, 28, 36-38)*

Mary and Joseph bring Jesus to the great Temple in Jerusalem, to the center of their faith, to present him there and have performed all the rites that first-born sons were accorded in those days.

The Jerusalem Temple wasn't some hushed, shadowy holy place, where people fell silent upon entering and mothers started pinching their children to get them to behave. At least the part of it that Mary and

Joseph would have been allowed into wasn't. Most of it would have been loud, chaotic, full of Gentiles and Jewish pilgrims from all over the place, priests and Temple workers, tour guides, people selling food, souvenirs, and animals for sacrifice.

Imagine poor countrified Joseph and Mary there in the big city, surrounded by all the noise and hubbub, wearing their backpacks on the front and extra travelers checks tucked into their shoes. Imagine their reaction when this crazy old dude runs up and snatches their baby from their arms. Never mind the ancient prophetess who starts yelling at all the passersby about them.

Why didn't they freak out and stop Simeon before he could even start singing? Maybe they had gotten into the habit of expecting this sort of thing, after all the angels and shepherds and stuff. Maybe this kind of thing happened to them even more often than the Bible reports.

Most of us aren't going to get the kind of supernatural attention that these guys got. But that doesn't mean you can't get in the habit of expecting to find blessings all around you. Once you get sensitized to something, you start seeing it everywhere, and the action of God is no different. You get used to it, then you come to expect it, and then you find out it's been going on all around you the whole time.

*God, teach me to expect your grace and to see it when it leaps out of the corners at me. Amen.*

# January 2

> "Now, master, let your servant go in peace according to your word, because my eyes have seen your salvation. You prepared this salvation in the presence of all peoples. It's a light for revelation to the Gentiles and a glory for your people Israel." (Luke 2:29-32)

Simeon had been told by the Holy Spirit that he wouldn't die until he had seen the long-awaited Messiah. This is the song he sings when he meets Jesus. They call it the *Nunc Dimittis,* which is how it begins if you translate it into Latin. With the whole "dismissing" thing, it's obviously the perfect way to end stuff. So it came to be used frequently to end worship services. And in places that had set prayers throughout the day, they used it at the end of the final service of the day as well.

It's easy to focus too much on the fulfillment and the praise in the song. But don't forget this wasn't only a hymn; it was also Simeon's swan song. The Bible doesn't say, but presumably, the next thing he does is die.

I hope you don't die tonight, but since it's the close of the day, you might as well make like a monk and ponder the mystery of the *Nunc Dimittis.* What would make you able to sing this song as fulsomely as Simeon did? What would make you so con-

# EVENING

tent, so pleased, that you could die happy in the moment after it happened? Seriously, what would make you able to say without exaggeration, "My eyes have seen your salvation"? And don't give me any pious bull about seeing God's salvation in the sunset or in the faces of every person you pass. I mean *tell me what actual thing would have to actually go down on the street in front of your house right-freaking-now* for you to say, and mean literally, that you have seen God's salvation?

I'm not saying it's gonna happen; I'm just saying it's worth picturing so you'll know it if you see it.

*God, I trust that your salvation is going on all around me, but if it's not too much trouble, I'd love to see it with my eyes. Amen.*

*Look! You will conceive and give birth to a son, and you will name him Jesus. (Luke 1:31)*

Lots of churches celebrate today as the Feast of the Holy Name of Jesus. It celebrates Jesus' official naming by his parents and is a time for meditating on that name. Apparently, over time some people decided just one name wasn't good enough, so they gave him some more and turned them into a litany many still pray today. Here's part of one:

> . . . brightness of eternal light
> King of glory
> sun of justice
> Son of the Virgin Mary
> most amiable
> most admirable
> the mighty God
> Father of the world to come
> angel of great counsel
> most powerful
> most patient
> most obedient
> meek and humble of heart
> lover of chastity

lover of us
God of peace
author of life
example of virtues
zealous lover of souls
our God
our refuge
father of the poor
treasure of the faithful
good Shepherd
true light
eternal wisdom
infinite goodness
our way and our life
joy of Angels
King of the Patriarchs
Master of the Apostles
teacher of the Evangelists
strength of Martyrs
light of Confessors
purity of Virgins
crown of Saints . . .

I know. Some of those get a little weird. But some of them are pretty great. And this is God we're talking about, so you should have to work for it a little, you know?

Which of these names can you just not handle? Why?

Which is your favorite? Why?

What names would you add? Today, take some time to write them down and do something beautiful with them: decorate them, illuminate them, calligraphy them, glitter them, ornament them. Put them where you'll see them often, and praise God's holy name.

*God, you are beautiful, and so is your name. Amen.*

*Listen to me, coastlands; pay attention, peoples far away. The LORD called me before my birth, called my name when I was in my mother's womb. (Isaiah 49:1)*

Names matter. What people call us, and what we call ourselves, matters.

What's the deal with your name? Who gave it to you? Why? What does it mean? Is there a story behind it? Are you named after someone? Are you glad to be that person's namesake?

Do you like your name?

Do you live up to it?

What about the names you give yourself? Why that e-mail address? Why that Twitter handle, that Instagram handle, that forum nickname?

Has somebody tried to force a name on you that you didn't want? That sweet, embarrassing nickname your parents called you? The mean thing the kids at the bus stop chanted? The thing your abusive ex used to call you?

Did you, once upon a time, decide to rename yourself? Did you change your name to "Daddy" or "Mommy"? Did you become somebody's "Schmoopie" or somebody's "Boo"?

# EVENING

Have you taken somebody else's name? Did you join a new family and decide to take on the head of the family's name? Did you change your name to "Christian"?

And did you know you have a name older than those? Sweeter than the ones crooned to you at bedtime, deeper than the ones that cut you to the quick? That matters more and tells the truth of you better than any of them? It's the name God gave to you in the womb, and every morning since: beloved.

Try to act like it, OK?

*Holy God, you gave me the only name that really matters.*
*I can't top that, but let me try just one more name that I think's*
*pretty good, too: just call me "yours." Amen.*

## January 4

*Then I looked on as the Lamb opened one of the seven seals. I heard one of the four living creatures say in a voice like thunder, "Come!" I looked on as he opened the sixth seal, and there was a great earthquake. The sun became ...*

*...black as funeral clothing, and the entire moon turned red as blood. The stars of the sky fell to the earth as a fig tree drops its fruit when shaken by a strong wind. The sky disappeared like a scroll being rolled up, and every mountain and island was moved from its place. (Revelation 6:1, 12-14)*

No, you're not stoned (though some have speculated that the author of this passage was). This is the Revelation to John, the book with far and away the trippiest visuals in the whole Bible. Feel weirded out? You should. It also contains a mighty whore, an evil dragon, a celestial mother with starry hair (she fights the dragon, naturally), giant insects, bowls full of plagues, hordes of angels, plus a new heaven and a new earth.

I know, I know. It's not your standard Christmas fare. But the deal with the church is that even when the waiting for the birth of Emmanuel is done, we still find ourselves waiting for everything else to be born again one day. And whether you like it or not, this is what the Christian tradition has to offer for a vision of our ultimate future.

What to make of it all? Obviously, it's about the end of everything you know. Beyond that, it's hard to tell. Some say it's a detailed plan for the "end times." Some say it's a coded diatribe against the Roman Empire. *I* say spending too much time thinking about it misses the point.

Better to just groove on the imagery. Think of it as some crazy artwork that regularly comes to life and rearranges itself. Don't analyze, just react. What do you feel when you imagine that rider on a pale horse? Or the angels swooping down to clothe the martyrs in white and mark the people for salvation? Sit with it. Stretch yourself. Spend some time imagining the unimaginable. And let it get you ready to ask yourself the real mind-bender: at the end of time, if all this comes to pass, how will it be good news?

(Hint: This is one book you might want to read the end of first.)

*O God, grant me good visuals. Show me a world beyond anything I can imagine. Make me ready to hope in things so wonderful only you could conceive them. Amen.*

Little children, it is the last hour. Just as you have heard that the antichrist is coming, so now many antichrists have appeared.... This person is the antichrist: the one who denies the Father and the Son. (1 John 2:18, 22)

Know what's super fun? Picturing the world as a giant battlefield on which the forces of good and evil are fighting it out.

Know what's even more fun? If the good and evil are personified by two people who can duke it out on behalf of the rest of us: Frodo and Sauron. Superman and Lex Luthor. Christ and antichrist.

The idea of a cosmic battle between titans, especially one in which we get to sit comfortably on the sidelines and watch, is appealing. It takes a truth we all know—that in some sense good and evil are at war in the world—and comfortably externalizes it. It turns it into a kind of play that we're totally into, but not in.

Lots of people tell the story of Jesus and "the antichrist" in just that way. The author of 1 John is not among them. The antichrist is not a single super-evil dude (and he's certainly not Satan's only-begotten son; you can thank the movies *Rosemary's Baby* and *The Omen* for that idea). Instead, he says, antichrists are everywhere—including the mirror. He says any time anyone denies the Parent, who is love, or the Son, who is Life, that person is antichrist.

It's that simple: deny love and life, and you're the antichrist. Embrace them, embody them, and you become like Christ. There's still a cosmic battle, just one being waged in your heart instead of in your adolescent fantasies.

It's a lot less fun than watching Harry Potter scrub Voldemort, but it's a battle in which winning is a lot more likely to save the world.

*God, I want giant eagles, superpowers, and Dumbledore on my side for this cosmic battle. But what I really need is you. Amen.*

# Christmas Calendar
## WEEK SIX

**5** Knock the media gods from their thrones; refuse to have any screen time tonight.

**6** Kneel down and sing a song to God today.

**January 5**

*Let the kings of Tarshish and the islands bring tribute; let the kings of Sheba and Seba present gifts. Let all the kings bow down before him; let all the nations serve him. (Psalm 72:10-11)*

If you have a true love, better spring for twelve drummers drumming, because tonight is the twelfth night of Christmas. Tomorrow begins Epiphany, the season of revelations, when one by one, the church retells the stories of the discovery of just who and what the baby born at Christmas is. The first revelation will come tomorrow, when the Gospel-writer Matthew says that wise men will bow before the baby. You might have heard that they were kings, which Matthew never mentions. If you have, it's probably because of this Psalm. Many years after the time of Jesus, commentators conflated the kings mentioned in the Psalm with the wise men from the Gospel. Then somebody wrote that song "We Three Kings," and the rest is history.

Twelfth Night traditions vary from place to place, but many of them share a common theme: inversion. Remembering the kings bowing down before a peasant child instead of King Herod, English sovereigns used to play the part of the fool on this evening, and someone else would take the throne and order them about.

Still today, some people celebrate with "king cakes" that have a small doll or other item baked into them. Whoever gets the piece with the insert becomes king or queen of the party.

So throw a Twelfth Night party tonight. We don't have a king, but there are still plenty of powers to knock down. Refuse to worship the media gods: turn off the TV and the computer and spend a whole night talking to somebody you share your house with. Refuse to bow down before the God of busy-ness: cancel an evening meeting and go have a drink with friends. Smash the god of respectability: stop being so darn well behaved and do something scandalous (or at least silly).

Tonight, take whatever powers usually rule your life, make them play the fool instead, and let the God of Love rule. After all, nobody worships Herod any more, but plenty of us worship a kid in a feedbox.

*God, in Jesus you turned the world upside down. Tonight, grant that we might do the same, and do it for you. Amen.*

January 5

After Jesus was born in Bethlehem in the territory of Judea during the rule of King Herod, magi came from the east to Jerusalem. They asked, "Where is the newborn king of the Jews? We've seen his star in the east, and we've come to honor him." ...

*...When King Herod heard this, he was troubled, and everyone in Jerusalem was troubled with him. (Matthew 2:1-3)*

Here's a thing you just can't get around: Christmas is, fundamentally, a threat.

Herod could tell you all about it. Like most kings, he's used to people paying him homage. He's used to bowing and scraping and "off with their heads" and all that. It's good to be the king.

Then the Magi come sailing into town, sparing him barely a glance, and ask where they might find a king worth bowing down to. You could almost feel bad for him, if he wasn't such a complete jerk.

The Christmas story is always a story of reversals. It's always a story of big shots being knocked down from their thrones. And by "big shots," I mean you. It's easy to believe that it's only wicked kings and scheming religious leaders that Jesus threatens. But they're not the only ones who get worshiped when they shouldn't.

# EVENING

Be honest: don't you spend most of your time thinking about your own fears and illnesses or celebrating your own intelligence and awesomeness or staring at your own griefs and insecurities, as if they were the most important things in the world? And isn't that pretty much the same as worshiping yourself?

Here's what Christmas does: it knocks you down off your high horse and offers you something worth worshiping. Something more powerful than your fear to tap into. Something more beautiful than your best to live your life by. Something more solid than your insecurities to secure yourself to.

All this might sound good to say, but if you're like the rest of us Herods, your ego is going to make it harder than you might expect to take it down from its throne. Give it a shot: tonight, spend thirty straight minutes thinking about God. Heck, don't even start there if you don't want to: just spend thirty minutes thinking about *anything other than yourself*. If you can do it, well done! If not, well then, it's time to start practicing.

*God, thank you for Christmas, for giving me something better than my own stuff to think about, and way better than myself to worship. Amen.*

## January 6

*Praise the LORD! Praise God in [God's] sanctuary! Praise God in [God's] fortress, the sky! (Psalm 150:1)*

When the ancients tilted their heads back and contemplated the night sky, they were filled with the same kind of wonder you are when you do the same thing. Which is why they thought God lived up there. Some of them made a science and an art out of stargazing, reveling in the beauty until they were convinced they could see meaning deep inside it. They were sometimes called magi; they say three of them followed a star all the way to Bethlehem.

But they hadn't seen nothin' yet. In 1990, the Hubble Space Telescope was launched by the modern descendants of the magi, to try to get a clearer look at the stars without the distorting effects of the earth's atmosphere. Take a minute right now and do a Google image search for "Hubble." Those are real. The universe *actually looks like that.* Just try to look at those images and not praise the Lord in the firmament.

I don't know about you, but staring at those images long enough freaks me right out. Contemplating the hugeness of the universe, the sheer amount of space out there, makes my mind feel like it's bending out of shape. Maybe the Hubble can stare at the stars indefinitely without earth's atmosphere in the way, but I'm pretty sure I couldn't without totally losing it. I need the distorting effects of the earth's atmosphere.

The wisest part of what the wise men did the day they came to honor Jesus was this: It realized that while praising God in the firmament is OK, praising God on earth is harder, and better.

*God, thanks for knowing that I just can't handle all that vastness. Thanks for risking distortion and showing up where we can see you. Amen.*

*They entered the house and saw the child with Mary his mother. Falling to their knees, they honored him. (Matthew 2:11)*

We're good at listing all the people we won't kneel before. We don't kneel for crowned heads. We don't bend for terrorists. By and large, we are a straight-backed, lock-kneed people.

Here is the way the three wise men were like us: they refused to kneel to Herod's crowned head. Here is the way we ought to be like the three wise men: they knew which things were not worth their homage and which things should drive them straight to their knees.

The wise men were wise, but God's no dummy, either. God knows there's one thing guaranteed to make just about anybody, even an American, kneel: a baby on the floor. I can remember my son's ninety-year-old great-grandmother diving straight to her knees to play with him on his little mat on the floor—even though it always took at least two of us to get her back up again later. I always think that inspiring that kind of delight and devotion has to be at least half the reason God decided to show up as a baby.

# EVENING

There's not much in the world that ought to be able to make you kneel. But this ought to: a deity with no place to lay his head, a savior who knelt before you to wash your feet, a God who could have remained above it all but stooped, bent, even groveled to get as close to you as possible and then paid a price for it.

Sometime today, do this: get down on your knees, open your arms out to your sides, and bow your head. Or if you're feeling especially brave, try touching your forehead to the floor. And don't you roll your eyes at me; you'd do this if the trainer at your gym told you to, wouldn't you? So get down there. If your body can't do these things, assume whatever posture speaks to you of humility and reverence.

Hold the position for a while, then sing:

*What can I give him, poor as I am?*
*If I were a shepherd, I would bring a lamb.*
*If I were a wise one, I would do my part.*
*Yet what I can I give him, give him my heart.*
*(the tune's "In the Bleak Midwinter"; Google it)*

*God, I wouldn't do this for anybody else but you. Well, and my yoga instructor, but you know what I mean. Amen.*

# EPILOGUE

See what happened there?

There you were back on December 1 standing in line, all huffy and bored and staring at your phone. Now look at you! Just a little over a month later, and here you are on your knees, crooning away to God. Or at least you're thinking about it.

This is just what Christmas will always do, if you let it. One minute, you're standing there wrapped in your own grumpy thoughts; the next, you're on your knees. Sometimes you're down there begging for help. Sometimes you're down there singing praises. Sometimes you're just trying to plug the tree in.

And sometimes, if you're lucky, you find yourself on your knees because there's a baby there. And she has a funny bald head and milk on her breath and drool on her chin and lights in her eyes. And even if you don't like babies, you can't help but get down there and look for just a second.

And now that God's gotten your attention, just a second is all God needs to give you what you really want.

# NOTES

**December 10: Evening**

*Gremlins.* Directed by Joe Dante. Universal City, CA: Amblin Entertainment, 1984. Film.

**December 13: Evening**

"Conversion of Paul." *Wikipedia: The Free Encyclopedia*. Retrieved October 18, 2009. http://en.wikipedia.org/w/index.php?title=Conversion_of_Paul&oldid=317179841.

**January 3: Morning**

"Catholic Prayer: Litany of the Most Holy Name of Jesus." Accessed April 15, 2014. https://www.catholicculture.org/culture/liturgicalyear/prayers/view.cfm?id=903.

**January 4: Morning**

George Bernard Shaw, among others; he called the book of Revelation "a curious record of the visions of a drug addict." See *Apocalyptic Thought in Early Christianity*, ed. Robert J. Daly (Grand Rapids: Baker Academic, 2009), 81–82.